62 TOURNAMENTS
32 COUNTRIES
06 CONTINENTS
01 ATP WORLD TOUR

REAL-TIME SCORING
LIVE STREAMING OF TOURNAMENTS
EXCLUSIVE HIGHLIGHTS & INTERVIEWS
WEEKLY FEATURES FROM ATP WORLD TOUR UNCOVERED
BEHIND-THE-SCENES FOOTAGE
IN-DEPTH PLAYER PROFILES
PREVIEWS & ANALYSIS
ALL AT THE OFFICIAL WEBSITE
www.ATPWorldTour.com

CONTENT, DESIGN AND PRINT

Advantage Media Network
Bridget Marrison,
Steph Peat, Mike Frey,
Lee Goodall, Andy Mountain

ATP CREDITS

Nanette Duxin, Kate Gordon,
LeAnn Silva, George Ciz,
Philippe Dore,
Paul Macpherson, Alex Romer

PHOTOGRAPHY

Images courtesy of
Getty Images, iStock,
Mike Frey and the
ATP World Tour tournaments

DATA

All information correct as
of 31 December 2009

ISBN: 1-907232-70-2

WELCOME

» The 2010 ATP World Tour season is underway, and fans are in for another action-packed year. Men's professional tennis is enjoying one of the most exciting periods in its history with the depth of talent on tour at an all-time high.

Last season, 19 of the top 20 players in the South African Airways ATP Rankings won at least one title, with Roger Federer regaining his No.1 position and earning the title of ATP World Tour Champion for the fifth time. With Rafael Nadal, Novak Djokovic, Andy Murray, Andy Roddick, Juan Martin Del Potro and Nikolay Davydenko, the Tour has a slew of bona fide stars competing for each and every title this season.

Who will be this year's breakout star? Only time will tell. The 2010 ATP World Tour comprises 62 tournaments in 32 countries, touching every corner of the globe, as players compete for valuable ranking points at ATP World Tour Masters 1000, 500 and 250 level tournaments, in addition to the four Grand Slams.

The season will conclude in November with the Barclays ATP World Tour Finals at The O2 in London for a second straight year, where the top eight singles players and doubles teams will battle it out for a chance to become the 2010 ATP World Tour Champion in singles and doubles. Last year over 250,000 fans attended the year-end championships, an all-time record for an indoor tournament.

Your 2010 ATP World Tour book contains a wealth of information about both established and up-and-coming players, as well as the tournaments happening every week across six continents. We hope this book will be a fun and useful resource for you throughout the year.

On behalf of the ATP, I would like to thank you for your continued support. We invite you to be part of this historic season by attending a live event, or following us on television and by visiting www.ATPWorldTour.com.

Sincerely,

Adam S. Helfant
ATP Executive Chairman & President

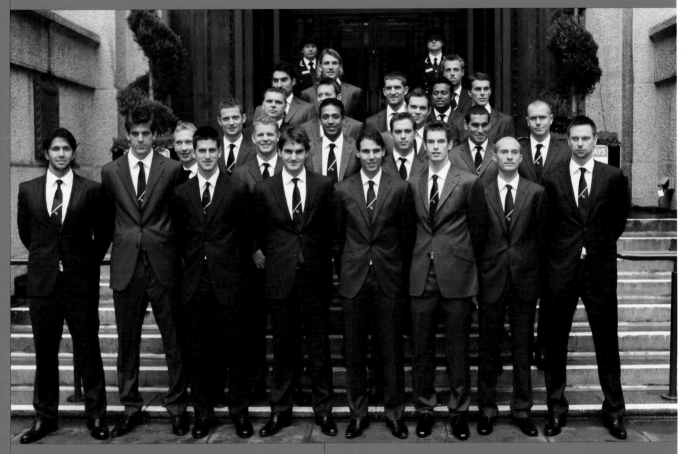

CONTENTS

6	HISTORY AND STRUCTURE
8	2009 IN PICTURES
14	2009 REVIEW
18	2009 IN NUMBERS
20	2009 BARCLAYS ATP WORLD TOUR FINALS
22	SINGLES PLAYER PROFILES
66	DOUBLES TEAMS PROFILES
74	2010 CALENDAR
76	TOURNAMENT PROFILES

ATP WORLD TOUR EXPLAINED

The superstars of the ATP World Tour will battle it out across six continents, in 32 countries and at 62 tournaments during 2010, all leading to the prestigious Barclays ATP World Tour Finals at The O2 in London...

Briton Andy Murray was one of 24 stars to feature at the Barclays ATP World Tour Finals in November 2009

In 2009 a new ATP World Tour tournament structure was created and the 2010 season will bear witness to the ongoing development of that same new framework of events.

The calendar is broken into three tiers – 40 ATP World Tour 250s, 11 ATP World Tour 500s and nine ATP World Tour Masters 1000s, all leading to the season-ending Barclays ATP World Tour Finals in London where the ATP World Tour Champion is crowned. In addition, the calendar also features a team event – the ARAG ATP World Team Championship – which takes place in Dusseldorf, Germany, every May.

The number next to the name of each level of event represents the points awarded to the winner in each respective tournament. At the end of the season, the top eight players with the most South African Airways 2010 ATP Rankings points will qualify for the season-ending championships, where players compete for a chance to be crowned 2010 ATP World Tour Champion.

Widespread stadia and infrastructure development took place during 2009 in leading cities including Madrid, Valencia, Beijing and Shanghai and the ATP World Tour will continue to keep working together with our tournaments to provide the most spectacular sporting stages. The players and fans will continue to benefit from further enhancements to tournament infrastructure across all tournament categories.

Once again, the tour is broken into several cohesive 'swings' which take place in specific regions of the world. Each of these is designed to build to a mini crescendo along the way to the season's grand finale in London. There is an uninterrupted European clay season, ending at the ATP World Tour Masters 1000 event in Madrid. The revamped Asian swing in the autumn ends at the ATP World Tour Masters 1000 event in Shanghai.

The climax to the season will once again take place in London where the top eight singles players and top eight doubles teams will battle it out at the Barclays ATP World Tour Finals, held at The O2 in November, at what will undoubtedly be another enthralling end to the season.

GRAND SLAM®
(2000 POINTS)

© Julian Finney/Getty Images

❝ The climax to the season will once again take place in London at the Barclays ATP World Tour Finals, held at The O2 ❞

》 Prior to 1968, Grand Slams and all other national championships were open to amateur competitors only, but two years later tournaments around the world formed a unified circuit, which became the Grand Prix, and in 1972 the leading pros joined forces to create the Association of Tennis Professionals (ATP). This direction marked another defining moment in the history of the ATP, when a handful of the game's leading players met in a stairwell at the US Open to discuss the need for a players' association. Under the leadership of newly-elected Executive Director Jack Kramer and President Cliff Drysdale, the ATP came to life with the goal of changing the game for the better.

One of the initial acts was the birth of a computer ranking system that provided fair analysis of a player's performance as well as an objective means to determine entries into tournaments. The ATP Rankings began on August 23 1973 and has continued as the official ranking system in men's tennis.

From 1974 to 1989, the men's circuit was administered by the Men's Tennis Council (MTC), made up of representatives of the International Tennis Federation (ITF), the ATP and tournament directors from around the world. Although the period during which the MTC guided the game was one of tremendous progress and improvement, players began to feel more and more that they should have a greater voice in their sport. Players had realised the time had come for them to take more control over the game.

At the 1988 US Open, ATP CEO Hamilton Jordan, surrounded by many of the top players in the game, held the now-famous "press conference in the parking lot". The ATP released "Tennis at the Crossroads" outlining the problems and opportunities facing men's tennis. One of the options available to the ATP was the formation of a new circuit, the ATP Tour.

Support for the new tour was quick as over 85 of the top 100 players signed a letter of support for a new system. Later, in the autumn of 1988, 24 players, including eight of the top 10, signed contracts to play the ATP Tour in 1990. Also that autumn tournament directors representing many of the world's leading events voiced their support for the players and joined them in what was to become a partnership unique in professional sports, with an equal voice in how the circuit is run. The 2010 season will mark the 21st year the ATP has administered the worldwide tour.

©Carl de souza/AFP/Getty Images

«
**Roger Federer collects the
ATP World Tour Champion
trophy for the fifth time in his
career at The O2 in London**

Gilles Simon tries Thai Boxing in Bangkok at the PTT Thailand Open, an event he went on to win

The Barclays ATP World Tour Finals competitors in relaxed mood before doing battle in London

©Valencia Open 500

©Clive Brunskill/Getty Images

The Valencia Open 500 was held inside the futuristic Agora building for the first time in November 2009

Bob and Mike Bryan were crowned ATP World Tour Doubles Champions for the fifth time in seven years

Russian Marat Safin says goodbye to his fans at the BNP Paribas Masters in Paris in November 2009

©Clive Rose/Getty Images

©Bertrand Guay/Getty Images

Frenchman Gael Monfils
shows why he is a fan
favourite all over the world

Roger Federer and Rafael
Nadal warm up in unusual
surroundings in Doha

2009 A YEAR TO REMEMBER...

A look back at the 2009 season and all its memorable moments...

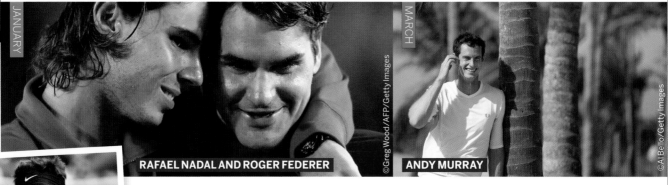

RAFAEL NADAL AND ROGER FEDERER

©Greg Wood/AFP/Getty Images

ANDY MURRAY

©Al Bello/Getty Images

JUAN MARTIN DEL POTRO

©Sandra Mu/Getty Images

JANUARY

》 The year exploded into life with titles for Radek Stepanek in Brisbane and Marin Cilic in Chennai while the Doha silverware went to Briton Andy Murray, who beat Andy Roddick in the final. The focus then immediately shifted to Australia and New Zealand where Juan Martin Del Potro tuned up for the first major of the year by winning the Heineken Open in Auckland, the fifth title of his career. Argentine David Nalbandian took the Medibank International in Sydney before the stars assembled in Melbourne for the first Grand Slam of the year, the Australian Open. Spain's Fernando Verdasco shocked Andy Murray and Jo-Wilfried Tsonga on his way to the semis and only an inspired Rafael Nadal could stop him, outlasting his friend in the event's longest ever match – five hours, 14 minutes – before surviving another five-setter against Roger Federer to win his sixth Grand Slam. While Rafa ruled the singles, Americans Bob and Mike Bryan won the doubles, their seventh Grand Slam trophy together.

FEBRUARY

》 Back on the ATP World Tour, a quintet of players were setting the pace, all five ending February with two trophies already on the shelf. Murray added the ATP World Tour 500 title in Rotterdam to his Doha crown, while Stepanek continued to astound, winning his second title in as many months in San Jose at the ripe old age of 30. Croatian Cilic continued his great form to capture his second pot of the year in Zagreb while Frenchman Tsonga and Spain's Tommy Robredo both hit some hot form to win two titles apiece in February.

MARCH

》 Onto March and the first two ATP World Tour Masters 1000s of the year, Indian Wells and Miami. Nadal continued his perfect start to the year by adding the BNP Paribas Masters title to his Australian Open crown, blowing away Murray in the final. Murray shrugged off the disappointment superbly, however, notching up wins over Verdasco, Del Potro and Novak Djokovic in the final of the Sony Ericsson Open in Miami for the third Masters 1000 shield of his career.

APRIL

》 By now the European clay court swing was around the corner and two former world No.1s got back to winning ways in early April. Spaniard Juan Carlos Ferrero captured his 12th title in Casablanca as the world No.115, while double Grand Slam champion from Australia, Lleyton Hewitt, bagged his 27th in Houston. Nadal enjoyed a fine run of form in April too, dominating once again on his favourite surface to win ATP World Tour Masters 1000s in Monte Carlo and Rome, with his fifth successive Barcelona Open Banco Sabadell title sandwiched inbetween.

JO-WILFRIED TSONGA

©Hamish Blair/Getty Images

JUAN CARLOS FERRERO

©Jasper Juinen/Getty Images

NENAD ZIMONJIC & DANIEL NESTOR

ROGER FEDERER

ROBIN SODERLING

MAY

》 Tomas Berdych, Albert Montanes and Djokovic all began May with a trophy, Djokovic's coming on home soil at the inaugural Serbia Open. The stars then assembled at the Mutua Madrileña Madrid Open and it was Federer who ended the week as champion after ending Nadal's streak of 33 wins on the 'dirt' in the final. Doubles team Daniel Nestor and Nenad Zimonjic had a great month too as they combined to win their fourth title in five events in Madrid, and the ARAG ATP World Team Championship went to Serbia after Viktor Troicki and Janko Tipsarevic combined to earn their country a 2-1 win over hosts Germany in the final.

JUNE

》 The month began with the world coming to terms with one of the biggest shocks for years when Sweden's Robin Soderling became the first player ever to beat Nadal at Roland Garros. Soderling's fourth round victory set the Swede on the way to his first Grand Slam final where he fell to a determined Federer. After three runners-up medals, the Swiss finally got his hands on the Paris trophy to become only the sixth player ever to complete a career Grand Slam. The title was doubly significant as it was Federer's 14th Grand Slam singles crown, drawing him level with American Pete Sampras. Once the clay had been dusted off their shoes, the men turned their attention to grass. Murray was quickly back to winning ways when he took the Queen's Club title in London, while Tommy Haas, Benjamin Becker and Dmitry Tursunov collected trophies in Halle, 's-Hertogenbosch and Eastbourne.

JULY

》 Murray's Queen's success raised British hopes of a home-grown Wimbledon champion and the Scot enjoyed his best ever result in SW19 when he reached the semis. In the last four he ran into an inspired Roddick, though, who booked his place in his third Wimbledon final against Federer. The Swiss had spent the first half of the year chasing Nadal at the top of the South African Airways 2009 ATP Rankings and when he edged a thrilling Wimbledon final 16-14 in the final set – the longest deciding set of any Grand Slam final – the Swiss returned to the top of the rankings, claimed a sixth Wimbledon trophy and surpassed Sampras with 15 Grand Slam titles. July was also significant for Nikolay Davydenko. A heel injury had restricted the Russian to just two events during the first three months of the year, but July saw him collect back-to-back titles in Hamburg and seven days later in Umag.

AUGUST

》 Early August witnessed the first signs that another big star was finding some form when Del Potro collected the sixth title of his career by beating Roddick to win the ATP World Tour 500 event in Washington DC. Del Potro had another fine week at the ATP World Tour Masters 1000 Canada too, reaching his first final at that level, but Murray proved too good on the day and the Scot was crowned champion. After Federer had notched up the 16th Masters 1000 of his illustrious career in Cincinnati, and later in the month Verdasco had claimed his third title in New Haven all eyes settled on New York, home to the final Grand Slam of the year.

JUAN MARTIN DEL POTRO

SEPTEMBER

NOVAK DJOKOVIC ©Matthew Stockman/Getty Images

ANDY MURRAY ©Julian Finney/Getty Images

OCTOBER

MARCOS BAGHDATIS ©Olivier Morin/AFP/Getty Images

OCTOBER

NIKOLAY DAVYDENKO ©Matthie Stockman/Getty Images

SEPTEMBER

❱❱ It was Federer who grabbed all the attention, gunning for his sixth successive title at Flushing Meadows and he looked to be peaking at just the right time as he beat Djokovic to reach the final. In the bottom half Del Potro was playing some astonishing tennis, though, beating Cilic and then Nadal to reach his first final at a major. Federer was in control when he took the opening set of the title decider, but Del Potro hit back to shock the defending champion in five to become the first Argentine to win in New York since Guillermo Vilas in 1977. Once the dust had settled, Montanes got back to winning ways with his second trophy of the season in Bucharest, while Gael Monfils won in Metz, Gilles Simon ruled in Bangkok and Davydenko grabbed his third title of 2009 in Kuala Lumpur as the Asian swing began.

OCTOBER

❱❱ The Asian swing came to a climax with simultaneous ATP World Tour 500s in Beijing and Tokyo followed by the inaugural Shanghai ATP Masters 1000. Tsonga grabbed his third title of the year in Japan, beating Russian Mikhail Youzhny in the final, while Djokovic got the better of an in-form Cilic in the Beijing final after the Croat had crushed Nadal in the semis. Onto Shanghai, and once again it was Davydenko who was in unstoppable form, this time beating Djokovic and Nadal in the semis and final respectively to claim the third ATP World Tour Masters 1000 of his career and put himself in contention for one of the remaining spots at the Barclays ATP World Tour Finals in London. The second half of October saw Cypriot Marcos Baghdatis return to the winner's circle in Stockholm, and there were also trophies for Youzhny on home turf in Moscow, Sergiy Stakhovsky in St. Petersburg, Jurgen Melzer in Vienna and Ivan Ljubicic in Lyon.

NOVEMBER

❱❱ The month began with the battle for the last two remaining spots at the year-end championships hotting up. Davydenko and Verdasco occupied seventh and eighth positions as simultaneous ATP World Tour 500s in Valencia and Basel got under way. The Valencia event, being played for the first time as an indoor tournament at its new home, the City of Arts and Sciences, went to Murray who claimed a career-best sixth title of his season, while Djokovic maintained his great form to beat Federer on home soil in Basel. The Serb went on to win back-to-back trophies in Paris a week later before the climax to the season, the Barclays ATP World Tour Finals, held for the first time in London. Federer, Del Potro, Davydenko and Soderling, who only made it to the event as a last-minute alternate, won through to the semi-finals and from there it was Davydenko who rose to the occasion, beating Federer for the first time in 13 attempts in the last four and outplaying Del Potro in the final to become the first Russian champion in the tournament's 40-year history. Despite losing in the semis, the week – and year – ended on a high for Federer, though, when he was crowned ATP World Tour Champion for the fifth time in his career. The doubles event was equally gripping with the Bryans ending their season in style by beating Max Mirnyi and Andy Ram in the final to claim their third season-ending championship title and grabbing the year-end No.1 ATP Doubles Team Ranking from Nenad Zimonjic and Daniel Nestor.

DECEMBER

❱❱ The competitive year ended with Spain defending their Davis Cup title in dominant fashion. A Spanish side featuring Rafael Nadal, David Ferrer, Fernando Verdasco and Feliciano Lopez crushed the Czech Republic 5-0 to claim the trophy for the fourth time since 2000.

2009 SINGLES AND DOUBLES CHAMPIONS

● ATP World Tour 250 ● ATP World Tour 500 ● ATP World Tour Masters 1000 ● Grand Slam Event ● Team Event ● Barclays ATP World Tour Finals ● Davis Cup

Week Starting	City	Event	Singles Champion	Doubles Champions
Jan 5	Doha	Qatar ExxonMobil Open	Andy Murray (GBR)	Rafael Nadal (ESP) & Marc Lopez (ESP)
Jan 5	Chennai	Aircel Chennai Open	Marin Cilic (CRO)	Rajeev Ram (USA) & Eric Butorac (USA)
Jan 5	Brisbane	Brisbane International	Radek Stepanek (CZE)	Jo-Wilfried Tsonga (FRA) & Marc Gicquel (FRA)
Jan 12	Sydney	Medibank International	David Nalbandian (ARG)	Mike Bryan (USA) & Bob Bryan (USA)
Jan 12	Auckland	Heineken Open	Juan Martin Del Potro (ARG)	Robert Lindstedt (SWE) & Martin Damm (CZE)
Jan 19	Melbourne	Australian Open	Rafael Nadal (ESP)	Mike Bryan (USA) & Bob Bryan (USA)
Feb 2	Zagreb	PBZ Zagreb Indoors	Marin Cilic (CRO)	Robert Lindstedt (SWE) & Martin Damm (CZE)
Feb 2	Vina Del Mar	Movistar Open	Fernando Gonzalez (CHI)	Brian Dabul (ARG) & Pablo Cuevas (URU)
Feb 2	Johannesburg	SA Tennis Open	Jo-Wilfried Tsonga (FRA)	Dick Norman (BEL) & James Cerretani (USA)
Feb 9	Costa do Sauipe	Brasil Open	Tommy Robredo (ESP)	Tommy Robredo (ESP) & Marcel Granollers (ESP)
Feb 9	Rotterdam	ABN AMRO World Tennis Tournament	Andy Murray (GBR)	Nenad Zimonjic (SRB) & Daniel Nestor (CAN)
Feb 9	San Jose	SAP Open	Radek Stepanek (CZE)	Radek Stepanek (CZE) & Tommy Haas (GER)
Feb 16	Marseille	Open 13	Jo-Wilfried Tsonga (FRA)	Michael Llodra (FRA) & Arnaud Clement (FRA)
Feb 16	Memphis	Regions Morgan Keegan Championships	Andy Roddick (USA)	Mark Knowles (BAH) & Mardy Fish (USA)
Feb 16	Buenos Aires	Copa Telmex	Tommy Robredo (ESP)	Alberto Martin (ESP) & Marcel Granollers (ESP)
Feb 23	Acapulco	Abierto Mexicano Telcel	Nicolas Almagro (ESP)	Michal Mertinak (SVK) & Frantisek Cermak (CZE)
Feb 23	Dubai	Barclays Dubai Tennis Championships	Novak Djokovic (SRB)	Dmitry Tursunov (RUS) & Rik De Voest (RSA)
Feb 23	Delray Beach	Delray Beach International Tennis Championships	Mardy Fish (USA)	Mike Bryan (USA) & Bob Bryan (USA)
Mar 2	Worldwide	Davis Cup First Round		
Mar 9	Indian Wells	BNP Paribas Open	Rafael Nadal (ESP)	Andy Roddick (USA) & Mardy Fish (USA)
Mar 23	Miami	Sony Ericsson Open	Andy Murray (GBR)	Andy Ram (ISR) & Max Mirnyi (BLR)
Apr 6	Casablanca	Grand Prix Hassan II	Juan Carlos Ferrero (ESP)	Oliver Marach (AUT) & Lukasz Kubot (POL)
Apr 6	Houston	US Men's Clay Court Championship	Lleyton Hewitt (AUS)	Mike Bryan (USA) & Bob Bryan (USA)
Apr 13	Monte-Carlo	Monte-Carlo Rolex Masters	Rafael Nadal (ESP)	Nenad Zimonjic (SRB) & Daniel Nestor (CAN)
Apr 20	Barcelona	Barcelona Open Banco Sabadell	Rafael Nadal (ESP)	Nenad Zimonjic (SRB) & Daniel Nestor (CAN)
Apr 27	Rome	Internazionali BNL d'Italia	Rafael Nadal (ESP)	Nenad Zimonjic (SRB) & Daniel Nestor (CAN)
May 4	Estoril	Estoril Open	Albert Montanes (ESP)	Scott Lipsky (USA) & Eric Butorac (USA)
May 4	Belgrade	Serbia Open	Novak Djokovic (SRB)	Oliver Marach (AUT) & Lukasz Kubot (POL)
May 4	Munich	BMW Open	Tomas Berdych (CZE)	Ivo Minar (CZE) & Jan Hernych (CZE)
May 11	Madrid	Mutua Madrileña Madrid Open	Roger Federer (SUI)	Nenad Zimonjic (SRB) & Daniel Nestor (CAN)
May 18	Kitzbuhel	Interwetten Austrian Open Kitzbuhel	Guillermo Garcia Lopez (ESP)	Andre Sa (BRA) & Marcelo Melo (BRA)
May 18	Dusseldorf	ARAG ATP World Team Championship	Serbia	
May 25	Paris	Roland Garros	Roger Federer (SUI)	Lukas Dlouhy (CZE) & Leander Paes (IND)
Jun 8	London	AEGON Championships	Andy Murray (GBR)	Mikhail Youzhny (RUS) & Wes Moodie (RSA)
Jun 8	Halle	Gerry Weber Open	Tommy Haas (GER)	Philipp Kohlschreiber (GER) & Christopher Kas (GER)
Jun 15	Eastbourne	AEGON International	Dmitry Tursunov (RUS)	Marcin Matkowski (POL) & Mariusz Fyrstenberg (POL)
Jun 15	's-Hertogenbosch	Ordina Open	Benjamin Becker (GER)	Dick Norman (BEL) & Wes Moodie (RSA)
Jun 22	London	Wimbledon	Roger Federer (SUI)	Nenad Zimonjic (SRB) & Daniel Nestor (CAN)
Jul 6	Newport	Campbell's Hall of Fame Tennis Championships	Rajeev Ram (USA)	Rajeev Ram (USA) & Jordan Kerr (AUS)
Jul 6	Worldwide	Davis Cup Quarterfinals		
Jul 13	Båstad	Catella Swedish Open	Robin Soderling (SWE)	Filip Polasek (SVK) & Jaroslav Levinsky (CZE)
Jul 13	Stuttgart	MercedesCup	Jeremy Chardy (FRA)	Michal Mertinak (SVK) & Frantisek Cermak (CZE)
Jul 20	Hamburg	International German Open	Nikolay Davydenko (RUS)	Paul Hanley (AUS) & Simon Aspelin (AUS)
Jul 20	Indianapolis	Indianapolis Tennis Championships	Robby Ginepri (USA)	Dmitry Tursunov (RUS) & Ernests Gulbis (LAT)
Jul 27	Los Angeles	LA Tennis Open	Sam Querrey (USA)	Mike Bryan (USA) & Bob Bryan (USA)
Jul 27	Gstaad	Allianz Suisse Open Gstaad	Thomaz Bellucci (BRA)	Michael Lammer (SUI) & Marco Chiudinelli (SUI)
Jul 27	Umag	ATP Studena Croatia Open Umag	Nikolay Davydenko (RUS)	Michal Mertinak (SVK) & Frantisek Cermak (CZE)
Aug 3	Washington DC	Legg Mason Tennis Classic	Juan Martin Del Potro (ARG)	Robert Lindstedt (SWE) & Martin Damm (CZE)
Aug 10	Montreal	Rogers Cup	Andy Murray (GBR)	Mark Knowles (BAH) & Mahesh Bhupathi (IND)
Aug 17	Cincinnati	Western & Southern Financial Group Masters	Roger Federer (SUI)	Nenad Zimonjic (SRB) & Daniel Nestor (CAN)
Aug 24	New Haven	Pilot Pen Tennis	Fernando Verdasco (ESP)	Jurgen Melzer (AUT) & Julian Knowle (AUT)
Aug 31	New York	US Open	Juan Martin Del Potro (ARG)	Lukas Dlouhy (CZE) & Leander Paes (IND)
Sep 14	Worldwide	Davis Cup Semifinals		
Sep 21	Bucharest	BCR Open Romania	Albert Montanes (ESP)	Michal Mertinak (SVK) & Frantisek Cermak (CZE)
Sep 21	Metz	Open de Moselle	Gael Monfils (FRA)	Ken Skupski (GRB) & Colin Fleming (GBR)
Sep 28	Kuala Lumpur	Proton Malaysian Open	Nikolay Davydenko (RUS)	Marcin Matkowski (POL) & Mariusz Fyrstenberg (POL)
Sep 28	Bangkok	PTT Thailand Open	Gilles Simon (FRA)	Rajeev Ram (USA) & Eric Butorac (USA)
Oct 5	Beijing	China Open	Novak Djokovic (SRB)	Bob Bryan (USA) & Mike Bryan (USA)
Oct 5	Tokyo	Rakuten Japan Open	Jo-Wilfried Tsonga (FRA)	Jurgen Melzer (AUT) & Julian Knowle (AUT)
Oct 12	Shanghai	Shanghai ATP Masters 1000 Presented by Rolex	Nikolay Davydenko (RUS)	Jo-Wilfried Tsonga (FRA) & Julien Benneteau (FRA)
Oct 19	Stockholm	If Stockholm Open	Marcos Baghdatis (CYP)	Kevin Ullyett (ZIM) & Bruno Soares (BRA)
Oct 19	Moscow	Kremlin Cup	Mikhail Youzhny (RUS)	Michal Mertinak (SVK) & Frantisek Cermak (CZE)
Oct 26	Lyon	Grand Prix de Tennis de Lyon	Ivan Ljubicic (CRO)	Nicolas Mahut (FRA) & Julien Benneteau (FRA)
Oct 26	St Petersburg	St. Petersburg Open	Sergiy Stakhovsky (UKR)	Ken Skupski (GRB) & Colin Fleming (GBR)
Oct 26	Vienna	Bank Austria TennisTrophy	Jurgen Melzer (AUT)	Oliver Marach (AUT) & Lukasz Kubot (POL)
Nov 2	Basel	Davidoff Swiss Indoors Basel	Novak Djokovic (SRB)	Nenad Zimonjic (SRB) & Daniel Nestor (CAN)
Nov 2	Valencia	Valencia Open 500	Andy Murray (GBR)	Michal Mertinak (SVK) & Frantisek Cermak (CZE)
Nov 9	Paris	BNP Paribas Masters	Novak Djokovic (SRB)	Nenad Zimonjic (SRB) & Daniel Nestor (CAN)
Nov 23	London	Barclays ATP World Tour Finals	Nikolay Davydenko (RUS)	Bob Bryan (USA) & Mike Bryan (USA)
Nov 30	Barcelona	2009 Davis Cup World Group Final	Spain	

*Grand Slams and Davis Cup are not ATP events.

2009 **BY NUMBERS**

With the dust settled on the 2009 season, we take a look
at the significant statistics behind the big stories

MOST TITLES WON

Name		Total	Indoor	Outdoor	Hard	Clay	Grass
1.	Andy Murray	6	2	4	5	0	1
=2.	Nikolay Davydenko	5	2	3	3	2	0
=2.	Novak Djokovic	5	2	3	4	1	0
=2.	Rafael Nadal	5	0	5	2	3	0
5.	Roger Federer	4	0	4	1	2	1
=6.	Juan Martin Del Potro	3	0	3	3	0	0
=6.	Jo-Wilfried Tsonga	3	1	2	3	0	0
=8.	Marin Cilic	2	1	1	2	0	0
=8.	Albert Montanes	2	0	2	0	2	0
=8.	Tommy Robredo	2	0	2	0	2	0
=8.	Radek Stepanek	2	1	1	2	0	0

LONGEST WINNING STREAKS

Player	Matches	Duration
Roger Federer	21	May 12-Aug 14
Rafael Nadal	17	April 12-May 17
Nikolay Davydenko	12	July 20-Aug 14
Andy Murray	12	Feb 9-Mar 22
Tommy Robredo	12	Feb 9-Feb 26
Novak Djokovic	11	Nov 2-Nov 25
Rafael Nadal	11	Jan 19-Feb 15
Juan Martin Del Potro	10	July 10-Aug 16
Tommy Haas	10	June 8-July 3
Andy Murray	10	June 8-July 3

OVERALL MATCH WIN LEADERS

Name	W-L	WINNING % IN 2009
1. Novak Djokovic	78-19	.804
2. Andy Murray	66-11	.857
3. Rafael Nadal	66-14	.825
4. Roger Federer	61-12	.836
5. Nikolay Davydenko	57-17	.770
6. Juan Martin Del Potro	54-16	.771
7. Jo-Wilfried Tsonga	53-20	.726
8. Fernando Verdasco	52-25	.675
9. Robin Soderling	49-21	.700
10. Andy Roddick	48-15	.762

DOUBLES 'MATCH TIE-BREAK' LEADERS

Name	W-L	%
Nestor-Zimonjic	14-6	(.700)
Kubot-Marach	14-7	(.667)
Bryan-Bryan	10-6	(.625)
Bhupathi-Knowles	11-7	(.611)
Melo-Sa	7-5	(.583)
Knowle-Melzer	13-10	(.565)
Fyrstenberg-Matkowski	9-7	(.563)
Cermak-Mertinak	13-12	(.520)
Mirnyi-A. Ram	6-6	(.500)
Damm-Lindstedt	6-8	(.462)

OVERALL SINGLES TIE-BREAK WIN LEADERS

Name	W-L	WINNING % IN 2009
1. Andy Roddick	33-12	.733
2. Jo-Wilfried Tsonga	33-17	.660
3. John Isner	27-12	.692
4. Roger Federer	26-11	.703
5. Juan Martin Del Potro	20-10	.667
6. Novak Djokovic	20-16	.556
7. Radek Stepanek	19-7	.731
8. Ivan Ljubicic	19-10	.655
9. Nikolay Davydenko	18-5	.783
10. Ivo Karlovic	18-27	.40

STATISTICAL LEADERS V TOP 10

Name	W-L	%
1. Andy Murray	14-6	.700
2. Roger Federer	15-10	.600
3. Nikolay Davydenko	9-6	.600
4. Mikhail Youzhny	4-3	.571
5. Rafael Nadal	14-11	.560
6. Novak Djokovic	15-12	.556
7. Juan Martin Del Potro	11-9	.550
8. Jo-Wilfried Tsonga	5-5	.500
9. John Isner	3-3	.500
10. Marin Cilic	4-5	.444

BAGELS OF THE YEAR (5)

There were five 'Double Bagels' in 2009...

- Juan Monaco bt Sergio Roitman, R1, Buenos Aires
- Robin Soderling bt Rainer Schuettler, RR, ARAG ATP World Team Championship, Düsseldorf
- Olivier Rochus bt Fernando Vicente, R1, Halle
- Robert Kendrick bt Vincent Spadea, R1, Los Angeles
- Novak Djokovic bt Jan Hernych, R2, Basel

FIRST-TIME ATP WORLD TOUR TITLE WINNERS

Player	Age	Tournament
Guillermo Garcia-Lopez	25	Kitzbuehel
Benjamin Becker	28	's-Hertogenbosch
Rajeev Ram	25	Newport
Jeremy Chardy	22	Stuttgart
Thomaz Bellucci	21	Gstaad

OVER-30 ATP WORLD TOUR TITLE WINNERS

Player	Tournament	Age
Tommy Haas	Halle	31 yrs, 2 mos.
Ivan Ljubicic	Lyon	30 yrs, 7 mos.
Radek Stepanek	Brisbane	30 yrs, 1 mos.
Radek Stepanek	San Jose	30 yrs, 2 mos.

YOUNGEST ATP WORLD TOUR TITLE WINNERS

Player	Tournament	Age
Marin Cilic	Chennai	20 yrs, 3 mos.
Juan Martin Del Potro	Auckland	20 yrs, 3 mos.
Marin Cilic	Zagreb	20 yrs, 4 mos.
Juan Martin Del Potro	Washington	20 yrs, 10 mos.
Juan Martin Del Potro	US Open	20 yrs, 11 mos.

YOUNGEST FINAL

Auckland – Juan Martin Del Potro (20) bt Sam Querrey (21)

OLDEST FINAL

San Jose – Radek Stepanek (30) bt Mardy Fish (27)
Casablanca – Juan Carlos Ferrero (29) bt Florent Serra (28)
Umag – Nikolay Davydenko (28) bt Juan Carlos Ferrero (29)

2009 RICOH
ATP WORLD TOUR
MATCHFACTS

ACES HIT

Rank	Name	Aces	Matches
1	Ivo Karlovic	890	43
2	Andy Roddick	762	61
3	Sam Querrey	739	64
4	Jo-Wilfried Tsonga	708	69
5	Roger Federer	657	71
6	John Isner	653	45
7	Ivan Ljubicic	636	55
8	Robin Soderling	586	68
9	Andy Murray	575	75
10	Juan Martin Del Potro	556	68

SERVICE GAMES WON

Rank	Name	%	Matches
1	Ivo Karlovic	92	43
2	Andy Roddick	91	61
3	Roger Federer	90	71
4	Jo-Wilfried Tsonga	89	69
5	John Isner	89	45
6	Fernando Gonzalez	88	55
7	Robin Soderling	86	68
8	Sam Querrey	86	64
9	Novak Djokovic	85	95
10	Andy Murray	85	75

POINTS WON RETURNING FIRST SERVE

Rank	Name	%	Matches
1	Andy Murray	35	75
2	Nikolay Davydenko	34	74
3	Juan Monaco	34	59
4	Novak Djokovic	33	95
5	Rafael Nadal	33	76
6	Marin Cilic	33	65
7	David Ferrer	32	62
8	Stanislas Wawrinka	32	48
9	Marcel Granollers	32	41
10	Fernando Verdasco	31	75

POINTS WON RETURNING SECOND SERVE

Rank	Name	%	Matches
1	Rafael Nadal	57	76
2	Andy Murray	56	75
3	David Ferrer	55	62
4	Novak Djokovic	54	95
5	Nikolay Davydenko	54	74
6	Fernando Verdasco	53	75
7	Juan Martin Del Potro	53	68
8	Radek Stepanek	53	63
9	Juan Monaco	53	59
10	Guillermo Garcia-Lopez	53	55

DOME SWEET DOME

© Julian Finney/Getty Images

Nikolay Davydenko was the last man standing at the 2009 Barclays ATP World Tour Finals. Lee Goodall looks back on a truly memorable week at The O2 in London

© Julian Finney/Getty Images

Eventual champion Nikolay Davydenko scored victories over all three of the year's Grand Slam champions on his way to victory in London

There are so many memorable aspects of the 2009 Barclays ATP World Tour Finals that it's difficult to know where to start. The breathtaking venue, the electric atmosphere inside the arena, the massive crowds that turned out for each of the 13 sessions, not to mention the drama on court. But, looking back, perhaps the lasting memory will be the level of tennis played by champion Nikolay Davydenko throughout the eight-day extravaganza, form that catapulted him to his first year-end championship title and well-deserved worldwide recognition. Although the 28-year-old from Volgograd began the eight-man singles and eight-team doubles event with a slight hiccup – a narrow round robin defeat to Serbia's Novak Djokovic (the man who beat him in the 2008 final in Shanghai) – the Russian rebounded superbly, going from strength to strength as the event thundered to a climax.

During the countdown to the star-studded tournament, held at The O2 in east London for the first of what will be a five-year residency, all the "will he, won't he" hype had surrounded Roger Federer, home hope Andy Murray and 2008 winner Djokovic. Most experts thought the champion would come from this trio. Davydenko had other ideas.

The Russian right-hander arrived in London in good shape and in fine form having collected four singles trophies – including the penultimate ATP World Tour Masters 1000 of the year in Shanghai – in the last five months. A heel injury had restricted Davydenko's activity to just two events in the first three months of 2009 but once he was back to full fitness he was dangerous against anyone.

Davydenko earned his first victory of the week when he edged out world No.2 Rafael Nadal in straight sets in a high-quality encounter in front of a packed house on Wednesday evening. Anyone who witnessed the closing passages of play during the second set tie-break might have sensed they were watching a player that was approaching the form of his life. The quality of court coverage and ball striking during those final baseline exchanges at times had to be seen to be believed.

With Nadal beaten, the Russian went into his final Group B contest knowing that victory over Robin Soderling would guarantee him a place in the semi-finals. It was far from easy, though. Having only made it to the event as an alternate after Andy Roddick's last-minute withdrawal, the powerful Swede was another playing the tennis of his career, form that had already earned him a semi-final spot thanks to wins against Djokovic and Nadal. Davydenko did just enough, however, digging out a draining 76(4) 46 63 victory that lasted over two hours.

Some late-night arithmetic 24 hours earlier had left world No.1 Roger Federer and US Open champion Juan Martin Del Potro as the top two players in Group A.

> **" In 2009, [it says] Davydenko forever on this trophy. For my name to be there is something amazing for me "**

Bob and Mike Bryan (right) captured the doubles title which earned them their fifth year-end No.1 ATP Doubles Team Ranking

The British public had been denied a home-grown semi-finalist by the narrowest of margins when Del Potro ended the round robin stages in second place in his group, ahead of Andy Murray by a whisker thanks to a better games-won percentage.

Davydenko's biggest challenge was still to come, however. Just 15 hours after waving goodbye to a capacity 17,500 crowd after beating Soderling, the Russian was back on court looking for his first victory in 13 attempts against the favourite for the crown, Federer.

On-court master of ceremonies Mark Petchey had joked during his interview with the Russian late on Friday that "no one beats you 13 times, right?" and, incredibly, he was right. Davydenko raised his levels once again and demonstrated supreme physical fitness to dig deep for a 62 46 75 victory to move into his second year-end championships final in as many years.

Another player steadily improving with each match at The O2 was Del Potro. His week had begun with him losing his opening round robin contest to Murray in three sets, before edging another two matches that went the distance against Fernando Verdasco and Federer. With Davydenko waiting in the final, Soderling and Del Potro went toe-to-toe for a ticket in Sunday's showpiece and the fans were treated to another cracker when the Argentine stopped the French Open finalist 67 63 76.

Buoyed by the confidence of his victory over Federer, Davydenko was unstoppable in Sunday's final, dominating Del Potro from the word go. In some ways it was his most straightforward outing of the week – victory coming in one hour and 24 minutes – but in real

terms the result represented Davydenko's finest hour as a professional. "In 2009, [it says] Davydenko forever on this trophy," the Russian said." For my name to be there is something amazing for me."

Amazing was the buzzword of the week. It summed up the venue as a whole, the drama inside what was a simply stunning arena, the size of the crowds and the standard of tennis throughout eight memorable days of competition. "Everything was perfect," said Davydenko, whose heroics made him the first ever Russian champion. "For sure we enjoy next year here in London."

Davydenko wasn't the only one to leave smiling. The American twins, Bob and Mike Bryan, also enjoyed a week to remember when they claimed the doubles title for the third time in their careers. Their 76(5) 63 victory over Belarussian Max Mirnyi and Andy Ram from Israel in the final was even more significant for the boys from California as it earned them the year-end No.1 ATP Doubles Team Ranking for the fifth time. Having begun the week needing to win the tournament to stand a chance of leapfrogging rivals Nenad Zimonjic from Serbia and Canada's Daniel Nestor, the climax to the doubles event couldn't have been any more dramatic. "To come full circle, do it in the last tournament, with so much riding on this one match, it's huge," said Mike Bryan. "We're going to be talking about this match for the rest of our lives."

Roger Federer reached the semi-finals and was crowned ATP World Tour Champion for the fifth time in his career

"Federer's goals for 2010 will be to defend his No.1 ranking and collect even more of the sport's major titles"

© Julian Finney/Getty Images

© Julian Finney/Getty Images

ROGER **FEDERER**

» **DATE OF BIRTH:** 8 August 1981 | **BORN:** Basel, Switzerland

Lives: Bottmingen, Switzerland

Height: 6'1" (185 cm)

Weight: 187 lbs (85 kg)

Style: Right-handed, one-handed backhand

Turned pro: 1998

Career singles titles: 61

ATP World Tour Masters 1000 titles: 16

Grand Slam titles: 15

Career-high South African Airways ATP Ranking: No.1 (Feb 04)

Career win-loss record: 678-161

Career prize money: $53,362,068

Career win-loss vs. top 10: 119-58

Barclays ATP World Tour Finals titles: 4

South African Airways 2009 ATP Ranking: No.1

Roger Federer admitted towards the end of 2009 that it had been his most emotional season as a professional tennis player. He began the year having to face the disappointment of losing his Australian Open crown but insisted there were more majors to come as he chased Pete Sampras' record haul of 14 Grand Slam singles titles. He was right.

In May he kick-started his year by winning the ATP World Tour Masters 1000 Madrid, which was held inside the brand new 'Magic Box' for the first time, and then went on to become only the sixth man in the sport's history to win the career Grand Slam of the four major championships by claiming his first Roland Garros title in Paris, a result that brought him level with Sampras.

The Swiss had begun the year as the world No.2 and climbing back to the top of the South African Airways 2009 ATP Rankings was another goal Federer had set himself. Despite his success at Roland Garros, Federer arrived at Wimbledon still as the world No.2 but two weeks later he had a record-breaking 15 Grand Slam singles titles to his name and once again was in pole position on top of the world rankings.

Federer's winning streak didn't stop there – he landed his 16th ATP World Tour Masters 1000 shield in Cincinnati and reached the final of the US Open where only an inspired Juan Martin Del Potro could stop him. His year on court ended in fine style with him qualifying for his eighth successive Barclays ATP World Tour Finals in London where, despite losing in the semi-finals, he was crowned 2009 ATP World Tour Champion for the fifth time in his career.

On a personal level 2009 was a year to remember too. Federer married his long-term girlfriend, Mirka, in April and the couple became parents to twin daughters, Charlene Riva and Myla Rose, in July.

The Mallorcan now has 15 ATP World Tour Masters 1000 titles and is third in the all-time Masters 1000 standings

RAFAEL **NADAL**

» DATE OF BIRTH: 3 June 1986 | **BORN:** Manacor, Mallorca, Spain

© Clive Rose/Getty Images

STATISTICS

Lives: Manacor, Mallorca, Spain

Height: 6'1" (185 cm)

Weight: 188 lbs (85 kg)

Style: Left-handed, two-handed backhand

Turned pro: 2001

Career singles titles: 36

ATP World Tour Masters 1000 titles: 15

Grand Slam titles: 6

Career-high South African Airways ATP Ranking: No.1 (Aug 08)

Career win-loss record: 401-91

Career prize money: $27,224,163

Career win-loss vs. top 10: 61-33

Barclays ATP World Tour Finals titles: 0

South African Airways 2009 ATP Ranking: No.2

Rafael Nadal may have struggled to maintain full fitness during 2009 but his achievements last season were still nothing short of outstanding. The powerful left-hander claimed his sixth Grand Slam title and his first on a hard court during a memorable Australian Open, winning back-to-back five-set matches against semi-final opponent Fernando Verdasco (the longest contest in the tournament's history at five hours and 14 minutes) and then his great rival Roger Federer in the final. In doing so, Nadal became the first Spaniard to win the Melbourne major and joined Jimmy Connors and Pete Sampras as one of only three players to have won three of the four Grand Slams before their 23rd birthday.

The Mallorcan also claimed his 13th, 14th and 15th ATP World Tour Masters 1000 titles in the first half of the year. His victories in Indian Wells, Monte-Carlo and Rome put him in third place on the ATP World Tour Masters 1000 titles won all-time leaderboard behind Federer on 16 and Andre Agassi on 17. He also won another trophy, in Barcelona, during the first half of 2009, form that meant he has now ended the season with at least five titles for the last five years.

His only disappointments were his surprise fourth-round exit at the French Open and being denied the chance to defend his Wimbledon crown because of tendinitis in both knees. Despite his battle with injury problems, though, Nadal also reached his second successive US Open semi-final, was runner-up at the Shanghai ATP Masters 1000 presented by Rolex and qualified for the Barclays ATP World Tour Finals in London for the fifth time in his career, ending the season as one of only three players to have won more than 60 matches during 2009. His year then ended on another high note when he was part of the Spanish team that claimed its second successive Davis Cup trophy on home soil in Barcelona.

"The Serbian won back-to-back titles in Basel and Paris towards the end of 2009, confidence-boosting form ahead of 2010"

©William West/AFP/Getty Images

©Michael Steele / Getty Images

NOVAK **DJOKOVIC**

» **DATE OF BIRTH:** 22 May 1987 | **BORN:** Belgrade, Serbia

STATISTICS

Lives: Monte Carlo, Monaco
Height: 6'2" (188cm)
Weight: 176 lbs (80 kg)
Style: Right-handed,
one-handed backhand
Turned Pro: 2003
Career singles titles: 16
ATP World Tour Masters 1000 titles: 5
Grand Slam titles: 1
**Career-high South African Airways
ATP Ranking:** No.3 (Jul 07)
Career win-loss record: 263-87
Career prize money: $15,984,098
Career win-loss vs. top 10: 35-42
Barclays ATP World Tour Finals titles: 1
**South African Airways
2009 ATP Ranking:** No.3

Having announced his arrival at the top of world tennis during 2008 when he won his first Grand Slam title in Melbourne in January and the end-of-year Tennis Masters Cup in November, Novak Djokovic was a picture of consistency during 2009, regularly featuring in the latter stages of major events on many different surfaces.

In fact, in some ways 2009 was his best year on tour. The right-hander from Belgrade reached a career-best 10 finals, winning five of those to land titles in Paris (his fifth ATP World Tour Masters 1000 trophy), three ATP World Tour 500s in Dubai, Beijing and Basel and another trophy on home soil at the inaugural Serbia Open in May.

Djokovic incredibly featured in another five finals during 2009 – including four ATP World Tour Masters 1000s in Miami, Monte-Carlo, Rome and Cincinnati – form that meant he surpassed 60 match wins for the third straight year and led the ATP World Tour in matches played (94), matches won (76) and hard court matches won (51), all personal bests.

Djokovic will be encouraged by his end-of-season form which is sure to fill him with confidence ahead of the new year. His results during the final quarter of 2009 included his Beijing title, a semi-final finish at the Shanghai ATP Masters 1000 presented by Rolex, before beating Roger Federer in his own backyard in Basel and then capturing the BNP Paribas Masters in Paris.

His year ended at the Barclays ATP World Tour Finals in London where he was making his third successive appearance at the end-of-season event. Djokovic may have failed to progress from the group stages at The O2 in London, but he was arguably the most consistent player on tour during 2009 and is sure to be in the running for more silverware once the new decade gets under way.

❝ Murray collected a career-best six titles in 2009 and was one of just three players to notch up more than 60 match wins throughout the year **❞**

© Jasper Juinen/Getty Images

© Tony Ashby/AFP/Getty Images

ANDY **MURRAY**

» DATE OF BIRTH: 15 May 1987 | **BORN:** Dunblane, Scotland

Lives: London, England
Height: 6'3" (190 cm)
Weight: 185 lbs (84 kg)
Style: Right-handed,
two-handed backhand
Turned pro: 2005
Career singles titles: 14
ATP World Tour Masters 1000 titles: 4
Grand Slam titles: 0
**Career-high South African Airways
ATP Ranking:** No.2 (Aug 09)
Career win-loss record: 221-76
Career prize money: $9,920,493
Career win-loss vs. top 10: 35-26
Barclays ATP World Tour Finals titles: 0
**South African Airways
2009 ATP Ranking:** No.4

It was a year of reaching new personal heights and breaking British records for Andy Murray during 2009, a period that saw him pick up a career-best six ATP World Tour singles titles during a very productive season. The right-hander from Scotland became the highest ranked British player ever when he ended the Roger Federer-Rafael Nadal four-year stronghold at the top of the South African Airways ATP Rankings, reaching a career-high of No.2 in mid-August.

He also became the first Briton since Bunny Austin in 1938 to win the pre-Wimbledon grass court title at the Queen's Club in London, and his victory at the Valencia Open 500 in November meant he has now won more titles than any other British player in the Open era – all this before his 23rd birthday.

Murray is considered by many to be one of the most intelligent match players around, and this, combined with his strength, sublime movement around the court and crisp ball striking, helped him collect trophies in all four corners of the world during 2009.

First it was in Doha where he dominated, then at the ATP World Tour 500 in Rotterdam, before ATP World Tour Masters 1000 successes in Miami and Canada, with that Queen's title sandwiched in between. He produced a personal best performance at his home Grand Slam, Wimbledon, too, where he reached the last four, and ended his season with more success in Valencia before appearing at the end-of-season Barclays ATP World Tour Finals for the second time in his career.

Murray's success on court is illustrated by the fact that he was one of just three players (with Nadal and Novak Djokovic) to notch up more than 60 match wins on tour between January and November 2009.

JUAN MARTIN **DEL POTRO** 🇦🇷

» DATE OF BIRTH: 23 September 1988 | **BORN:** Tandil, Argentina

Lives: Tandil, Argentina
Height: 6'6" (198 cm)
Weight: 182 lbs (83 kg)
Style: Right-handed, two-handed backhand
Turned pro: 2005
Career singles titles: 7
ATP World Tour Masters 1000 titles: 0
Grand Slam titles: 1
Career-high South African Airways ATP Ranking: No.5 (Apr 09)
Career win-loss record: 138-69
Career prize money: $6,679,875
Career win-loss vs. top 10: 17-28
Barclays ATP World Tour Finals titles: 0
South African Airways 2009 ATP Ranking: No.5

The 'Tower of Tandil' has emerged as one of the most exciting young players on the ATP World Tour and he shocked international sport by claiming his first Grand Slam title at Flushing Meadows in September 2009. Del Potro's play at the US Open reached new levels, scoring back-to-back victories over Rafael Nadal in the semi-finals and Roger Federer in the final, the first time anyone has beaten those two players at the same major.

His victory in New York made him a household name in his native Argentina, as he became the first player from the country to win the US Open since the great Guillermo Vilas in 1977. The scale of his popularity was in no doubt whatsoever when 40,000 fans greeted him on his return to his hometown of Tandil – a third of the population.

Del Potro first made a splash on the ATP World Tour by winning four successive titles during the summer of 2008 and the powerful right-hander added another three during 2009 – trophies in Auckland and Washington DC, as well as his US Open success. Del Potro also featured in his first ATP World Tour Masters 1000 final in Canada and qualified for the season-ending Barclays ATP World Tour Finals in London.

Del Potro's level of play to beat Federer in the group stages of the end-of-season event showed everyone that his first major title in New York was no fluke. He qualified for the semi-finals in London where he toppled Sweden's Robin Soderling, before falling to red hot Russian Nikolay Davydenko in the final. Despite the defeat, his tennis during the week made him lots of new friends in the UK.

❝ Del Potro became the first player from Argentina to win the US Open since Guillermo Vilas in 1977 ❞

NIKOLAY **DAVYDENKO**

» DATE OF BIRTH: 2 June 1981 | **BORN:** Severodonezk, Ukraine

STATISTICS

Lives: Volgograd, Russia

Height: 5'10" (178 cm)

Weight: 154 lbs (70 kg)

Style: Right-handed, two-handed backhand

Turned pro: 1999

Career singles titles: 19

ATP World Tour Masters 1000 titles: 3

Grand Slam titles: 0

Career-high South African Airways ATP Ranking: No.3 (Nov 06)

Career win-loss record: 375-230

Career prize money: $13,239,499

Career win-loss vs. top 10: 31-49

Barclays ATP World Tour Finals titles: 1

South African Airways 2009 ATP Ranking: No.6

The Russian is widely regarded as one of the most difficult players to break down thanks to his speed around the court, aggressive baseline game and mental toughness, and he proved that by becoming the first Russian to win the Barclays ATP World Tour Finals in London in 2009.

Davydenko has been at the top of the rankings for some time – he peaked at a career-high of No.3 in 2006 during a year in which he made the last eight at the Australian and French Opens and the semi-finals at Flushing Meadows. The right-hander has finished in the top ten for the last five seasons, a statistic that demonstrates his consistency at the very top of the game.

The 2009 season began slowly after a heel injury restricted Davydenko to just two tournaments in the first three months, but once he was back to full fitness the Russian was one of the hottest players on tour. He won four titles in four months in Hamburg, Umag, Kuala Lumpur and Shanghai before making it a high five for the year when he claimed the biggest title of his career by bagging the end-of-season Barclays ATP World Tour finals. The Russian admitted he had never once been asked for his autograph in the English capital, but all that changed after his heroics at The O2 arena, where he beat every one of the season's Grand Slam champions including his first ever success over Roger Federer.

> **Davydenko has finished inside the world's top ten for the last five seasons**

©Clive Brunskill/Getty Images

©Ian Walton/Getty Images

©Clive Brunskill/Getty Images

ANDY **RODDICK**

» DATE OF BIRTH: 30 August 1982 | **BORN:** Omaha, Nebraska, USA

STATISTICS

Lives: Austin, Texas, USA

Height: 6'2" (188 cm)

Weight: 195 lbs (88 kg)

Style: Right-handed, two-handed backhand

Turned pro: 2000

Career singles titles: 27

ATP World Tour Masters 1000 titles: 4

Grand Slam titles: 1

Career-high South African Airways ATP Ranking: No.1 (Nov 03)

Career win-loss record: 507-163

Career prize money: $17,109,084

Career win-loss vs. top 10: 31-56

Barclays ATP World Tour Finals titles: 0

South African Airways 2009 ATP Ranking: No.7

Andy Roddick is a former world No.1, having climbed to the top of the rankings in 2003, the same year he won his first Grand Slam title, the US Open, and the Texas resident has been one of the world's best tennis players for nearly a decade after finishing in the top ten for the last eight seasons.

Roddick featured in one of the most memorable major finals ever during 2009, an epic with Roger Federer at Wimbledon that was eventually settled when the Swiss edged the longest deciding set in Grand Slam final history 16-14 after over four hours on court. Roddick's performances to beat home favourite Andy Murray in the semi-finals and stretch Federer to five fantastic sets 48 hours later made him many new fans around the globe. While the heartbreak of his defeat in the final was there for all to see – he lost serve just once in the entire match, in the very last game – the man with the biggest serve in the world once again proved that he is a serious contender on the sport's biggest stages by reaching his third Wimledon final.

The popular American, who married Brooklyn Decker in April 2009, once again qualified for the season-ending championships, held in London for the first time, but a knee injury forced him to withdraw from the event at the last minute. Roddick can be confident that when he does finally return to Great Britain he will receive a hero's welcome after his Wimbledon performances.

> **" Andy played his part in one of the most memorable Grand Slam finals of all time during the summer of 2009 "**

ROBIN **SODERLING**

» DATE OF BIRTH: 14 August 1984 | **BORN:** Tibro, Sweden

STATISTICS

Lives: Monte Carlo, Monaco

Height: 6'4" (193 cm)

Weight: 192 lbs (87 kg)

Style: Right-handed, two-handed backhand

Turned pro: 2001

Career singles titles: 4

ATP World Tour Masters 1000 titles: 0

Grand Slam titles: 0

Career-high South African Airways ATP Ranking: No.8 (Nov 09)

Career win-loss record: 215-139

Career prize money: $5,367,761

Career win-loss vs. top 10: 18-40

Barclays ATP World Tour Finals titles: 0

South African Airways 2009 ATP Ranking: No.8

The quiet Swede became a superstar the world over on May 31 2009 when he became the first player ever to beat four-time defending champion Rafael Nadal on the clay of Roland Garros – an achievement many thought was an impossible task in tennis. That victory came in the fourth round and the man from Tibro went from strength to strength thereafter, playing some of the best tennis of his career during his stay in Paris to add David Ferrer, Nikolay Davydenko and Fernando Gonzalez to his list of victims before falling to Roger Federer in his first Grand Slam final appearance.

Soderling then went on to prove his form at the French major was no fluke by achieving personal bests at Wimbledon, where he reached the fourth round, and also at the US Open, where he made the last eight. He also won his first title on clay in 2009, on home soil at the SkiStar Swedish Open in Bastad, and ended his year in style by reaching the semi-finals on his debut at the Barclays ATP World Tour Finals in London, a run of form that left him at a career-high ranking of No.8.

❝ The Swede is now a superstar after achieving what many thought was the impossible – beating Rafael Nadal in Paris ❞

FERNANDO **VERDASCO**

PLAYER PROFILES

STATISTICS

Lives: Madrid, Spain

Height: 6'2" (188 cm)

Weight: 179 lbs (81 kg)

Style: Left-handed, two-handed backhand

Turned pro: 2001

Career singles titles: 3

ATP World Tour Masters 1000 titles: 0

Grand Slam titles: 0

Career-high South African Airways ATP Ranking: No.7 (Apr 09)

Career win-loss record: 239-173

Career prize money: $5,319,180

Career win-loss vs. top 10: 9-45

Barclays ATP World Tour Final titles: 0

South African Airways 2009 ATP Ranking: No.9

©Clive Brunskill/Getty Images

The left-hander from Madrid has always been one of the most explosive ball strikers in men's tennis and he reached new heights during a career-best 2009 season. After helping Spain win the Davis Cup in Argentina in December 2008 – Verdasco hit the winning shot at the end of a five-set victory over Jose Acasuso – the Spaniard went off to work on his fitness during the off season with Andre Agassi's former trainer, Gil Reyes, and seemed to return as a different player in January 2009.

The left-hander was one of the men to beat during the first few tournaments of the new season. Verdasco, who many say has the biggest forehand in the game, reached the final in Brisbane, then produced some memorable tennis to reach the last four of the Australian Open, seeing off the likes of Andy Murray and Jo-Wilfried Tsonga along the way. In the semi-finals he took on fellow Spaniard and eventual champion Rafael Nadal in one of the most memorable matches of recent years. Their five-set marathon featured some brutal baseline play from both men and Nadal emerged from the longest ever match at the Melbourne major – five hours and 14 minutes of magical tennis – by the skin of his teeth.

Verdasco also hit a new ranking high during 2009 when he peaked at No.7 in April, and picked up the third title of his career in New Haven in the summer before ending the year by making his debut at the Barclays ATP World Tour Finals in London.

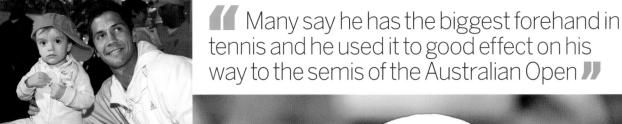

❝ Many say he has the biggest forehand in tennis and he used it to good effect on his way to the semis of the Australian Open ❞

©Stan Honda/AFP/Getty Images

©Matthew Stockman/Getty Images

JO-WILFRIED **TSONGA**

» **DATE OF BIRTH:** 17 April 1985 | **BORN:** Le Mans, France

Lives:	Gingins, Switzerland
Height:	6'2" (188 cm)
Weight:	200 lbs (91 kg)
Style:	Right-handed, two-handed backhand
Turned pro:	2004
Career singles titles:	5
ATP World Tour Masters 1000 titles:	1
Grand Slam titles:	0
Career-high South African Airways ATP Ranking:	No.6 (Nov 08)
Career win-loss record:	103-47
Career prize money:	$3,960,164
Career win-loss vs. top 10:	14-14
Barclays ATP World Tour Final titles:	0
South African Airways 2009 ATP Ranking:	No.10

Having been named the ATP Newcomer of the Year in 2007, Jo-Wilfried Tsonga wasted no time in establishing himself among the game's elite during 2008.

The explosive Frenchman blasted his way into his first Grand Slam final in Melbourne, won his first ATP World Tour Masters 1000 shield on home soil in Paris, qualified for the year-end Tennis Masters Cup in Shanghai and reached a career-high ranking of No.6 at the end of what was a remarkable season. In many ways, his achievements that year are all the more incredible given he missed three months of competitive play after undergoing knee surgery in May.

Tsonga's brand of high-energy, acrobatic, thrilling tennis – he is one of the few players around who is regularly willing to come forward to finish points off from the net – has made him one of the most popular men on the ATP World Tour and 2009 will go down as another successful season for the Le Mans-born right-hander.

Tsonga, who is a former junior world No.2, produced consistent results during 2009 from the first month until the last, form that enabled him to claim a career-best three titles in Johannesburg, Marseille and his first ATP World Tour 500 trophy in Tokyo in October. Over the last couple of years Tsonga has established himself as the French No.1 and is sure to be in the running for more silverware in 2010.

❝ His brand of high-energy, acrobatic, attacking tennis has made him one of the most popular players in the world ❞

> Gonzalez ended 2009 at No.11 in the rankings – four places higher than his listing at the start of the season

© Julian Finney/Getty Images

FERNANDO **GONZALEZ**

» DATE OF BIRTH: 29 July 1980 | **BORN:** Santiago, Chile

Lives: Santiago, Chile	
Height: 6'0" (183 cm)	
Weight: 180 lbs (82 kg)	
Style: Right-handed, one-handed backhand	
Turned pro: 1999	
Career singles titles: 11	
ATP World Tour Masters 1000 titles: 0	
Grand Slam titles: 0	
Career-high South African Airways ATP Ranking: No.5 (Jan 07)	
Career win-loss record: 349-184	
Career prize money: $8,306,045	
Career win-loss vs. top 10: 27-47	
Barclays ATP World Tour Final titles: 0	
South African Airways 2009 ATP Ranking: No.11	

The fiery Chilean has one of the biggest forehands around and has used it to very good effect over the years, climbing to as high as No.5 in the world rankings back in 2007 when he also reached his first Grand Slam final in Melbourne. As well as an impressive ATP World Tour record – he has 11 singles titles to his name – the South American's Olympic performances have been nothing short of remarkable.

At the Athens Games in 2004 he claimed bronze in the singles and gold in the doubles alongside Nicolas Massu, performing a double escape act in both of his medal matches. Gonzo, as he is known, saved two match points in his bronze medal play-off to outlast American Taylor Dent 16-14 in the third set. He and Massu incredibly then fought off four match points to beat Germany's Nicolas Kiefer and Rainer Schuettler in the doubles gold medal match. And as if that wasn't enough, in 2008 he left Beijing with a singles silver medal after

beating American James Blake 11-9 in the third set of their semi-final before losing to Spain's Rafael Nadal in the final.

As well as a clay court title on home soil in Chile – the 11th trophy of his career – his form in 2009 enabled him to reach the semi-finals in Barcelona, Rome and at the French Open too where only an inspired Robin Soderling could stop him. His results at Roland Garros meant he re-entered the top ten for the first time in nearly a year and he ended 2009 at No.11, four places higher than his ranking at the start of the season.

©Matthew Stockman/Getty Images

©AFP/Getty Images

©Samul Kabani/AFP/Getty Images

©Nick Laham/Getty Images

RADEK **STEPANEK**

» **DATE OF BIRTH:** 27 November 1978 | **BORN:** Karvina, Czech Republic

STATISTICS

Lives: Monte Carlo, Monaco
Height: 6'1" (185 cm)
Weight: 167 lbs (76 kg)
Style: Right-handed, two-handed backhand
Turned pro: 1996
Career singles titles: 4
ATP World Tour Masters 1000 titles: 0
Grand Slam titles: 0
Career-high South African Airways ATP Ranking: No.8 (Jul 06)
Career win-loss record: 258-179
Career prize money: $6,166,282
Career win-loss vs. top 10: 21-43
Barclays ATP World Tour Final titles: 0
South African Airways 2009 ATP Ranking: No.12

Radek Stepanek, the oldest player in the top 20 at the end of 2009, will remember his year on tour for a remarkable start to his season and some red hot form for the Czech Republic in the Davis Cup. The right-hander, known by many for his 'worm' on-court celebratory dance routine, won his third and fourth career titles inside two months in Brisbane and San Jose at the start of 2009. In Australia, in January, he blew away the likes of Sweden's Robin Soderling, Frenchman Richard Gasquet and in-form Spaniard Fernando Verdasco to lift the Brisbane trophy and at the beginning of February he repeated his title-winning form in California during a run that included a victory over top-tenner Andy Roddick.

His Davis Cup form for the Czech Republic during 2009 was arguably even more impressive, though. He clinched victory for his nation over France in the first round of the World Group with a win over another top ten player, Gilles Simon, beat Juan Monaco in the deciding rubber against Argentina in the quarter-finals and outlasted Ivo Karlovic 16-14 in the fifth set to set the Czechs on their way to a 4-1 semi-final success over Croatia.

Stepanek's highest-ever ranking of No.8 came back in 2006, a season that included his first ever singles title in Rotterdam, a runner-up finish at the ATP World Tour Masters 1000 on clay in Hamburg and an appearance in the quarter-finals at Wimbledon, his best ever Grand Slam performance to date.

❛❛ The Czech was the oldest player inside the top 20 at the end of 2009 having picked up his third and fourth titles during the season ❜❜

GAEL **MONFILS**

STATISTICS

PLAYER PROFILES

Lives: Nyon, Switzerland

Height: 6'4" (193 cm)

Weight: 177 lbs (80 kg)

Style: Right-handed, two-handed backhand

Turned pro: 2004

Career singles titles: 2

ATP World Tour Masters 1000 titles: 0

Grand Slam titles: 0

Career-high South African Airways ATP Ranking: No.9 (Mar 09)

Career win-loss record: 141-100

Career prize money: $3,539,442

Career win-loss vs. top 10: 14-26

Barclays ATP World Tour Final titles: 0

South African Airways 2009 ATP Ranking: No.13

L ike many of the flamboyant Frenchmen that have thrilled tennis audiences before him, Gael Monfils' brand of athletic, attacking tennis attracts huge numbers of fans wherever he goes in the world.

He should be used to the attention, though, given he was one of the hottest prospects in tennis as a youngster after winning the boys' singles at the Australian Open, Roland Garros and Wimbledon before ending his junior days as the world No.1. Lamonf, as he's known on tour, then made the transition to the senior game look frighteningly easy when he won his first ATP World Tour title in 2005 aged just 18, the same year he was named ATP Newcomer of the Year.

Monfils teamed up with Australian coach Roger Rasheed in July 2008 and made his debut in the world's top ten in late February 2009 after a sensational start to the year when he reached the semi-finals in Doha, beating world No.1 Rafael Nadal along the way, the last 16 at the Australian Open, the semi-finals in Rotterdam and was runner-up on clay in Acapulco, the Dutch and Mexican tournaments both ATP World Tour 500 events. Those results pushed him up to a career-high ranking of No.9 in the world in March.

Later in the year he notched up the second title of his career in September when he won indoors in Metz and ended his year on a high by reaching his first ATP World Tour Masters 1000 final in Paris in November, where he narrowly lost to world No.3 Novak Djokovic.

" Monfils had a memorable 2009 – he broke into the top ten and won the second title of his career in Metz "

MARIN **CILIC**

» DATE OF BIRTH: 28 September 1988 | **BORN:** Medjugorje, Bosnia & Herzegovia

Lives: Monte Carlo, Monaco
Height: 6'6" (198 cm)
Weight: 180 lbs (82 kg)
Style: Right-handed, two-handed backhand
Turned pro: 2005
Career singles titles: 3
ATP World Tour Masters 1000 titles: 0
Grand Slam titles: 0
Career-high South African Airways ATP Ranking: No.13 (May 09)
Career win-loss record: 104-71
Career prize money: $2,201,350
Career win-loss vs. top 10: 8-15
Barclays ATP World Tour Final titles: 0
South African Airways 2009 ATP Ranking: No.14

"Cilic is the latest talented, entertaining player to come out of Croatia and reached a career-best ranking of No.13 during 2009"

Marin Cilic is the latest in a long line of talented, entertaining players to come out of Croatia, and probably the country's most famous tennis export, Goran Ivanisevic, had a hand in his development. The 2001 Wimbledon champion asked his former coach, Australian Bob Brett, to assess Cilic's potential as a 15-year-old and the two men have been working together ever since.

Cilic enjoyed his best year on tour during 2009 when he claimed two titles, reached a career-high ranking of No.13 and finished the season with his best year-end listing of No.14. The silverware came early in the year in Chennai and indoors in Zagreb, but arguably his finest moment came at the US Open when he beat world No.2 Andy Murray on his way to the quarter-finals, his best Grand Slam result so far. Cilic continued to improve as the year matured, scoring a thumping victory over Rafael Nadal on his way to a runners-up finish in Beijing in October before another appearance in a final in Vienna later the same month.

GILLES **SIMON**

» DATE OF BIRTH: 27 December 1984 | **BORN:** Nice, France

STATISTICS

Lives: Neuchatel, Switzerland

Height: 5'11" (180 cm)

Weight: 152 lbs (69 kg)

Style: Right-handed, two-handed backhand

Turned pro: 2002

Career singles titles: 6

ATP World Tour Masters 1000 titles: 0

Grand Slam titles: 0

Career-high South African Airways ATP Ranking: No.6 (Jan 09)

Career win-loss record: 161-113

Career prize money: $3,685,120

Career win-loss vs. top 10: 10-23

Barclays ATP World Tour Final titles: 0

South African Airways 2009 ATP Ranking: No.15

Since turning professional in 2002, Gilles Simon has proved he is one of the toughest opponents around on the ATP World Tour thanks to the devastating pace he creates with his groundstrokes – particularly his world-class backhand – his speed around the court and his endurance. The last of those qualities was demonstrated during his 2008 season when he led the statistics with 14 match wins having lost the first set.

His best year on tour so far came that same year when he won three titles – Bucharest, Indianapolis and Casablanca – and qualified for the year-end ATP Masters Cup in Shanghai where he beat Roger Federer in the group stages to qualify for the semi-finals.

That year he was one of only three players to beat the world's top three of Federer, Rafael Nadal and Novak Djokovic in the same season and also broke into the top ten for the first time after reaching his first ATP World Tour Masters 1000 final in Madrid. His semi-final at the Spanish event was particularly memorable, when he outlasted Nadal in front of the Spaniard's home fans in a match that lasted just short of three-and-a-half hours.

Simon continued to pass personal milestones in 2009 – he reached a career-high ranking of No.6 in January and produced his best Grand Slam performance to date by making the last eight at the Australian Open in Melbourne where he beat Mario Ancic and Marin Cilic along the way. In September he began his Asian swing in style by collecting the sixth title of his career in Bangkok where he beat Serbia's Viktor Troicki in the title decider and dropped just one set all week.

❝❞ Simon continued to pass personal milestones in 2009, reaching a career-high ranking of No.6 and winning his sixth title ❞❞

TOMMY **ROBREDO**

» DATE OF BIRTH: 1 May 1982 | **BORN:** Hostalric, Spain

STATISTICS

Lives: San Cugat del Valles, Spain
Height: 5'11" (180 cm)
Weight: 165 lbs (75 kg)
Style: Right-handed, one-handed backhand
Turned pro: 1998
Career singles titles: 9
ATP World Tour Masters 1000 titles: 1
Grand Slam titles: 0
Career-high South African Airways ATP Ranking: No.5 (Aug 06)
Career win-loss record: 377-228
Career prize money: $8,074,007
Career win-loss vs. top 10: 15-63
Barclays ATP World Tour Final titles: 0
South African Airways 2009 ATP Ranking: No.16

A solid baseline game and a fine tactical tennis brain have made Tommy Robredo undoubtedly one of the best clay courters in the world on his day but he is also one Spaniard who can perform well on all surfaces, perhaps as a result of his upbringing, developing his game on the hard courts of the Olot Swimming Club before first playing on the 'dirt' at the Spanish Federation Tennis Center in Barcelona aged 14.

The gutsy right-hander has been as high as No.5 in the world back in 2006, a season in which he won two titles, including his first ever ATP World Tour Masters 1000 shield in Hamburg, Germany.

Robredo has won at least one title in his last four seasons and he began 2009 in fantastic form, reaching the semi-finals at Vina del Mar in Chile, before collecting back-to-back clay court trophies in Costa do Sauipe, Brazil, and Argentine capital Buenos Aires in February. During that period he compiled a 12-match winning streak and won 14 of 16 matches during the four-week Latin American clay court swing, before later going on to reach the last eight at the French Open, form that enabled him to end the season at No.16, five places higher than his January listing.

The right-hander, who was named by his tennis coach parents after the musical by the British rock band, The Who, was honoured by the Spanish Tennis Journalists Association at the end of the 2009 season when he was awarded the Fair Play prize in recognition of his sportsmanship on and off court. Earlier in the year, the Spaniard created a new foundation providing support to disabled players and organised a new wheelchair tennis tournament.

❝ Robredo began 2009 in fantastic form, claiming back-to-back titles and winning 14 of 16 matches during the South American swing **❞**

©Clive Brunskill/Getty Images

DAVID **FERRER**

STATISTICS

Lives: Valencia, Spain

Height: 5'9" (175 cm)

Weight: 160 lbs (73 kg)

Style: Right-handed,
two-handed backhand

Turned pro: 2000

Career singles titles: 7

ATP World Tour Masters 1000 titles: 0

Grand Slam titles: 0

**Career-high South African Airways
ATP Ranking:** No.4 (Feb 08)

Career win-loss record: 293-188

Career prize money: $6,932,489

Career win-loss vs. top 10: 21-40

Barclays ATP World Tour Final titles: 0

**South African Airways
2009 ATP Ranking:** No.17

One of the most intense, gutsy players on the ATP World Tour, David Ferrer is another Spaniard who has worked hard at performing to a high level on every surface and his record since turning pro in 2000 reflects that. The right-hander enjoyed an incredible season in 2007 when he won three titles, reached the semi-finals at the US Open, and qualified for his first year-end Tennis Masters Cup in Shanghai where he won four out of five matches and ended the week as runner-up to Roger Federer. Early the next year, after reaching the last eight at the Australian Open, Ferrer peaked at a career-high world ranking of No.4 in February 2008.

Although he failed to add to his career tally of seven singles titles, 2009 will still go down as another solid season on tour. The Valencia resident reached two ATP World Tour 500 finals in Dubai and Barcelona, another two semi-finals and won both his singles, including a five-set victory over Radek Stepanek, during Spain's 5-0 victory against the Czech Republic in the Davis Cup final in December.

❝ The Valencia resident reached two ATP World Tour 500 finals in 2009 and won both his singles for Spain in the Davis Cup final **❞**

TOMMY **HAAS**

>> **DATE OF BIRTH:** 3 April 1978 | **BORN:** Hamburg, Germany

STATISTICS

Lives: Bradenton, Florida, USA

Height: 6'2" (188 cm)

Weight: 195 lbs (88 kg)

Style: Right-handed, one-handed backhand

Turned Pro: 1996

ATP World Tour titles: 12

ATP World Tour Masters 1000 titles: 1

Grand Slam titles: 0

Career-high South African Airways ATP Ranking: No.2 (May 02)

Career win-loss record: 459-251

Career prize money: $9,910,081

Career win-loss vs. top 10: 40-67

Barclays ATP World Tour Final titles: 0

South African Airways 2009 ATP Ranking: No.18

Tommy Haas has enjoyed a long and illustrious career but even now, in his early thirties, he can still compete with the best players in the world and enjoyed something of a resurgence during 2009. His results during the season enabled him to finish the year as the 18th best player on the planet – 66 places higher than his end-of-season ranking a year earlier.

Haas, who won a silver medal at the 2000 Sydney Olympics and reached No.2 in the world rankings in 2002, showed at Roland Garros and Wimbledon just how dangerous he is. In Paris he came within a whisker of beating eventual champion Roger Federer in the fourth round when he led the Swiss by two sets to love and held a break point at 4-3 in the third set.

Federer hit back from the brink to win that match in five sets, but Haas then showed how adaptable his game is by switching surfaces with ease. He carried his form into the grass court season when he went on to win the 12th title of his career in Halle, beating Serbia's Novak Djokovic in the final.

Immediately after the German tournament, he then produced his best Wimbledon performance to date when he outplayed the likes of Marin Cilic, Igor Andreev and Djokovic for the second time inside a month on his way to the semi-finals where, once again, it was only a red-hot Federer who could end his run. Despite the defeat, Haas had featured in the fourth Grand Slam semi-final of his career aged 31 and ended the season as the German No.1.

" Haas climbed 66 places in the rankings during the 2009 season "

©Glyn Kirk/AFP/Getty Images

©Lars Baron/Getty Images

MIKHAIL **YOUZHNY**

» **DATE OF BIRTH:** 25 June 1982 | **BORN:** Moscow, Russia

Lives: Moscow, Russia

Height: 6'0" (183 cm)

Weight: 160 lbs (73 kg)

Style: Right-handed, one-handed backhand

Turned pro: 1999

Career singles titles: 5

ATP World Tour Masters 1000 titles: 0

Grand Slam titles: 0

Career-high South African Airways ATP Ranking: No.8 (Jan 08)

Career win-loss record: 296-225

Career prize money: $6,164,083

Career win-loss vs. top 10: 23-51

Barclays ATP World Tour Final titles: 0

South African Airways 2009 ATP Ranking: No.19

Mikhail Youzhny – the man with the military-style victory salute and one of the best single-handed backhands in the business – will be remembered by many for his incredible victory over Paul-Henri Mathieu in the 2002 France-Russia final of the Davis Cup in Paris. The Muscovite trailed the Frenchman by two sets to love in the deciding rubber but dramatically hit back to win the match in five sets and deliver the famous team trophy back home to Russia.

As well as a Davis Cup winner, Youzhny is also a former top ten player – he peaked at a career-high listing of No.8 back in January 2008 – and is also a Grand Slam semi-finalist after making the last four in New York in 2006. His run to the semis at Flushing Meadows four years ago featured victories over David Ferrer, Tommy Robredo and Rafael Nadal before Andy Roddick stopped him in four sets.

After a slow start to the 2009 season, the right-hander started to find some of his best form towards the end of the year. He reached the final at the ATP World Tour 500 tournament in Tokyo, beating three seeds along the way, then won his home-town tournament in Moscow before reaching his third final in four events in Valencia where he beat Gilles Simon and Nikolay Davydenko before losing to Great Britain's Andy Murray. Youzhny's ranking rise during 2009 was very impressive – between July and November he shot up 53 places to leave himself inside the top 20 at year-end. The Russian should be full of confidence at the start of the 2010 season.

❚❚ The Muscovite has enjoyed success at the highest level of the game – he is a former Grand Slam semi-finalist and top ten player ❚❚

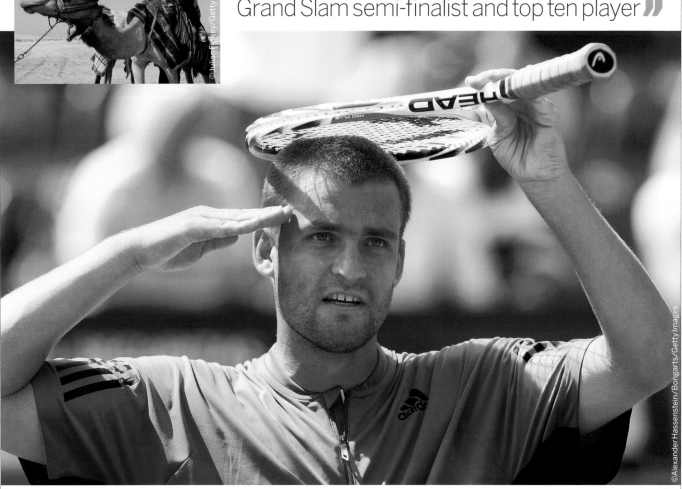

TOMAS **BERDYCH**

» DATE OF BIRTH: 17 September 1985 | **BORN:** Valasske Mezirici, Czech Republic

STATISTICS

Lives: Monte Carlo, Monaco	
Height: 6'5'' (196 cm)	
Weight: 200 lbs (91 kg)	
Style: Right-handed, two-handed backhand	
Turned pro: 2002	
ATP World Tour titles: 5	
ATP World Tour Masters 1000 titles: 1	
Grand Slam titles: 0	
Career-high South African Airways ATP Ranking: No.9 (Aug 07)	
Career win-loss record: 217-142	
Career prize money: $5,068,088	
Career win-loss vs. top 10: 14-41	
Barclays ATP World Tour Final titles: 0	
South African Airways 2009 ATP Ranking: No.20	

Since winning his first ATP World Tour title in 2004, Tomas Berdych has established himself among the world's best players, ending each of the last four seasons inside the world's top 20. Comfortable on slow courts – two of his five ATP World Tour titles have come on clay courts – the 6ft 5'' Czech right-hander is also dangerous on faster surfaces, particularly when his big serve is firing on all cylinders.

Berdych is one of only a handful of active players who can boast an ATP World Tour Masters 1000 trophy after capturing the BNP Paribas Masters in Paris in 2005, producing five successive victories over top 20 players along the way, including a five-set win over Croatia's Ivan Ljubicic in the final.

Arguably his best season to date, however, came in 2007 when he used his big game to good effect on grass to pick up the Halle title before producing what is still his best Grand Slam performance in reaching the last eight at Wimbledon. Later that summer he peaked at a career-high ranking of No.9.

Berdych has won at least one title for the last three seasons and it was in Munich on clay where he collected more singles silverware in 2009. He also featured strongly in the Czech Republic's run to the final of the 2009 Davis Cup, winning singles rubbers in the first round, quarter-finals and semi-finals against France, Argentina and Croatia respectively.

> **The Czech right-hander has won at least one title for the last three seasons and his latest came on clay in Munich in 2009**

" Wawrinka played his part in a gripping late-night, five-set thriller against Andy Murray under the brand new Centre Court roof "

©Mark Kolbe/Getty Images

STANISLAS **WAWRINKA**

» **DATE OF BIRTH:** 28 March 1985 | **BORN:** Lausanne, Switzerland

STATISTICS

Lives: St. Barthelemy, Switzerland	
Height: 6'0" (183 cm)	
Weight: 174 lbs (79 kg)	
Style: Right-handed, one-handed backhand	
Turned pro: 2002	
Career singles titles: 1	
ATP World Tour Masters 1000 titles: 0	
Grand Slam titles: 0	
Career-high South African Airways ATP Ranking: No.9 (Jun 08)	
Career win-loss record: 141-116	
Career prize money: $3,156,132	
Career win-loss vs. top 10: 11-29	
Barclays ATP World Tour Final titles: 0	
South African Airways 2009 ATP Ranking: No.21	

This likeable Swiss has been forced to spend most of his career in the shadow of world No.1 compatriot Roger Federer, but has emerged in recent years as a superstar in his own right.

Stan, as he's known to his friends, famously teamed up with Federer to win a doubles gold medal at the Beijing Olympics in August 2008, beating multi-Grand Slam doubles champions the Bryan brothers in the semi-finals and Swedes Simon Aspelin and Thomas Johansson in the final. The same summer Wawrinka enjoyed a personal high on the singles court too when he peaked at a career-best ranking of No.9 following his first appearance in the final of an ATP World Tour Masters 1000 on clay in Rome.

Wawrinka's highlights during 2009 included beating Federer in Monte Carlo on his way to the semi-finals, fourth round finishes at ATP World Tour Masters 1000s in Indian Wells and Miami and a gripping late-night defeat to Andy Murray in the fourth round at Wimbledon, the first full contest to be played under the Centre Court's retractable roof that was unveiled at the 2009 Championships.

It's not just Olympic medals Wawrinka and Federer will be able to compare before long, since the right-hander from Lausanne is to become a father in early 2010. Once he has become accustomed to the challenges of parenting the former French Open junior champion will be keen to add to the one ATP World Tour singles title he so far owns, which came on clay in Umag in 2006.

©William West/Getty Images

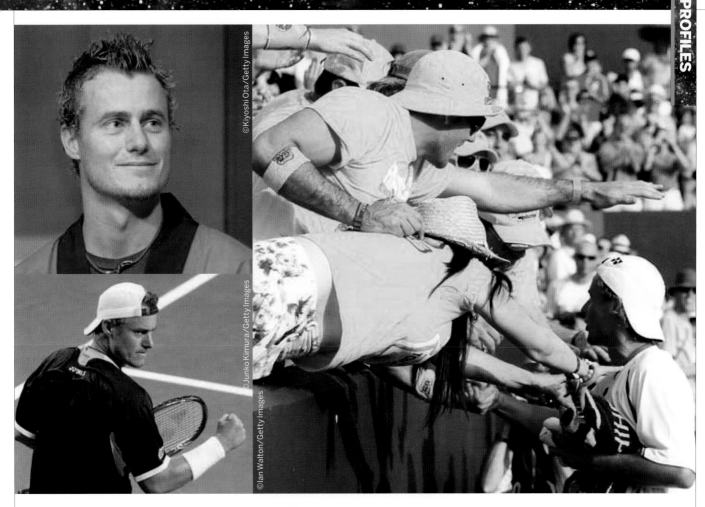

LLEYTON **HEWITT**

» **DATE OF BIRTH:** 24 February 1981 | **BORN:** Adelaide, Australia

STATISTICS

Lives: Nassau, Bahamas	
Height: 5'11" (180 cm)	
Weight: 170 lbs (77 kg)	
Style: Right-handed, two-handed backhand	
Turned pro: 1998	
Career singles titles: 27	
ATP World Tour Masters 1000 titles: 2	
Grand Slam titles: 2	
Career-high South African Airways ATP Ranking: No.1 (Nov 01)	
Career win-loss record: 520-181	
Career prize money: $18,312,036	
Career win-loss vs. top 10: 59-56	
Barclays ATP World Tour Final titles: 2	
South African Airways 2009 ATP Ranking: No.22	

This Australian, known the world over for his gutsy, never-say-die attitude on court, is now considered one of the veterans of the ATP World Tour having achieved almost all there is to achieve as a professional tennis player.

Hewitt is a former world No.1 – he was the youngest year-end No.1 at just 20 years old back in 2001 – a two-time Grand Slam champion after winning in New York in 2001 and at Wimbledon a year later, a two-time Tennis Masters Cup champion and he has twice been part of a winning Davis Cup team in 1999 and 2003. As well as all that, Hewitt has also tasted success at ATP World Tour Masters 1000 level having won the Indian Wells event back-to-back in 2002 and 2003 and he had notched up an impressive 27 singles trophies by the end of the 2009 season.

The father of two spent most of 2009 battling his way back to full fitness after undergoing hip surgery in August 2008. His results during the last 12 months were admirable and showed that despite going under the knife he can still compete with the best players in the world. He dropped out of the top 100 for the first time in over ten years in February 2009, but once again showed his grit and determination to climb back to the top in style, winning the 27th title of his career in Houston and reaching the last four at ATP World Tour 500 events in Memphis and Tokyo as well as a quarter-final finish at Wimbledon to end the year just outside the top 20.

> **Hewitt spent 2009 proving his full fitness following hip surgery and hit back in style to end the season just outside the top 20**

JUAN CARLOS **FERRERO**

» **DATE OF BIRTH:** 12 February 1980 | **BORN:** Onteniente, Spain

STATISTICS

Lives: Villena, Spain

Height: 6'0" (183 cm)

Weight: 160 lbs (73 kg)

Style: Right-handed, two-handed backhand

Turned pro: 1998

Career singles titles: 12

ATP World Tour Masters 1000 titles: 4

Grand Slam titles: 1

Career-high South African Airways ATP Ranking: No.1 (Sep 03)

Career win-loss record: 421-225

Career prize money: $12,588,898

Career win-loss vs. top 10: 38-55

Barclays ATP World Tour Final Titles: 0

South African Airways 2009 ATP Ranking: No.23

From the moment Juan Carlos Ferrero won his first ATP World Tour title in only his second season as a professional in Mallorca in 1999, it was clear he was a special talent. That same year he was named ATP Newcomer of the Year and just four years later he won his first Grand Slam title, the French Open, followed that up by finishing runner-up at the US Open and reached the summit of the South African Airways ATP rankings in September the same year.

In 2009 the Spaniard produced some world class tennis, picking up the 12th singles title of his career on clay in Casablanca in April, reaching the final in Umag in July and climbing over 90 places in the rankings between May, when he was outside the top 100, and December to end the year inside the top 25 for the eighth time in ten years.

As well as an astute tennis brain, incredible speed around the court (his nickname is Mosquito) and one of the most fearsome forehands in the business, Ferrero is also known for his interests off court. In 2001 he opened his own tennis school, Juan Carlos Ferrero-Equelite Tennis Academy, in his hometown of Villena, Alicante, and in 2007 became a hotel owner when he finished refurbishing Hotel Ferrero in Bocairente, an hour south of Valencia. The Spaniard is also the co-owner of the Valencia Open, an ATP World Tour 500 event that re-located to the futuristic surroundings of the City of Arts and Sciences in November 2009.

©Matthew Stockman/Getty Images

©Hamish Blair/Getty Images

" Ferrero won the 12th title of his career in Casablanca in 2009 and climbed over 90 ranking spots between May and December "

IVAN **LJUBICIC**

» DATE OF BIRTH: 19 March 1979 | **BORN:** Banja Luka, Bosnia & Herzegovia

Lives: Monte Carlo, Monaco

Height: 6'4" (193 cm)

Weight: 202 lbs (92 kg)

Style: Right-handed, one-handed backhand

Turned pro: 1998

Career singles titles: 9

ATP World Tour Masters 1000 titles: 0

Grand Slam titles: 0

Career-high South African Airways ATP Ranking: No.3 (May 06)

Career win-loss record: 375-252

Career prize money: $8,037,929

Career win-loss vs. top 10: 34-60

Barclays ATP World Tour Final titles: 0

South African Airways 2009 ATP Ranking: No.24

> **❝** Ljubicic won the Lyon title in 2009, making him one of only three thirtysomethings to win singles trophies during the year **❞**

D espite being one of the older players towards the top of the South African Airways ATP rankings, Ivan Ljubicic showed his younger peers a thing or two by reaching eight quarter-finals or better during 2009 before ending his season in style, capturing the ninth title of his career when he won the Lyon indoor event without dropping a set. In doing so, the former world No.3 joined Tommy Haas and Radek Stepanek to become one of only three thirtysomethings to win an ATP World Tour singles trophy last season.

The tall right-hander has enjoyed considerable success on court over the years. He is a former French Open semi-finalist and claimed an Olympic doubles bronze medal with Mario Ancic in Athens in 2004. His record in Davis Cup is arguably even more impressive – Ljubicic led the Croatian team to the World Group title in 2005 when he won 11 out of 12 matches during the campaign.

Ljubicic is also well known for his generosity towards others off court. He served on the ATP Player Council between 2002 and 2008 and was elected as the European player representative on the ATP Board in August 2008. The Croat was also named the 2007 ATP Arthur Ashe Humanitarian of the Year for his work with the Special Olympics. His most recent accolade came in December 2009 when he was named an ambassador for Special Olympics Monaco, whose mission is the integration of the mentally handicapped through sport.

©Stephen Dunn/Getty Images

SAM **QUERREY**

» DATE OF BIRTH: 7 October 1987 | **BORN:** San Francisco, CA, USA

STATISTICS

Lives: Santa Monica, CA, USA

Height: 6'6" (198 cm)

Weight: 200 lbs (91 kg)

Style: Right-handed, two-handed backhand

Turned pro: 2006

Career singles titles: 2

ATP World Tour Masters 1000 titles: 0

Grand Slam titles: 0

Career-high South African Airways ATP Ranking: No.22 (Aug 09)

Career win-loss record: 94-82

Career prize money: $1,730,172

Career win-loss vs. top 10: 6-22

Barclays ATP World Tour Final titles: 0

South African Airways 2009 ATP Ranking: No.25

The 6ft 6" American is one of the tallest players on the ATP World Tour so it's little wonder he rates his forehand and serve as his biggest weapons. The Californian has used them to good effect during the four years he has so far spent on tour, collecting two singles titles along the way. His first came in his home state, on the hard courts of Los Angeles in 2008, and he returned to the tournament a year later to successfully defend his title.

The 2009 season was Querrey's finest by some margin – as well as his second Los Angeles trophy, he reached another four finals during 11 months of competition. The first came early, in Auckland in January, and midway through the year he hit a patch of red-hot form, reaching three successive finals on home soil in Newport, Indianapolis

and LA. He then clinched the 2009 US Open Series at Pilot Pen Tennis, in New Haven, where he finished runner-up to Spain's Fernando Verdasco, a result that earned him a new career-high South African Airways ATP ranking of No.22 in August. His year came to a premature end, however, when he injured his right arm in Bangkok when a glass table he was sitting on collapsed.

©Jared Wickerham/Getty Images

" The American hit a patch of red-hot form in the summer of 2009 when he reached three successive finals on home soil **"**

NICOLAS **ALMAGRO**

» DATE OF BIRTH: 21 August 1985 | **BORN:** Murcia, Spain

STATISTICS

Lives: Murcia, Spain

Height: 6'0" (183 cm)

Weight: 179 lbs (81 kg)

Style: Right-handed, one-handed backhand

Turned pro: 2003

Career singles titles: 5

ATP World Tour Masters 1000 titles: 0

Grand Slam titles: 0

Career-high South African Airways ATP Ranking: No.11 (Jul 08)

Career win-loss record: 142-118

Career prize money: $3,062,456

Career win-loss vs. top 10: 7-19

Barclays ATP World Tour Final titles: 0

South African Airways 2009 ATP Ranking: No.26

This powerful Spanish baseliner from Murcia considers his best surface to be clay and it's not hard to understand why given he has won all of his five ATP World Tour singles titles on the 'dirt'. His game from the back of the court is highly effective – he keeps opponents on the back foot with venomous groundstrokes and a vicious kick serve (one of the most potent in the world) and this weaponry has helped him collect silverware twice on home soil in Valencia (in 2006 and 2007, before the tournament moved indoors), once on the Brazilian clay of Costa Do Sauipe (2008) and twice in Acapulco, the most recent of those Mexican titles coming in February 2009 when he beat French world No.10 Gael Monfils in the final.

The 2008 season was Almagro's best yet, a year during which he collected three of his five singles titles, reached another final in Valencia and enjoyed a run to the quarter-finals at Roland Garros, his best Grand Slam performance to date. His form during the first half of that year pushed him to the brink of the top ten when he peaked at No.11 in July.

His tennis during 2009 was equally consistent, helping him reach six quarter-finals or better and finish inside the top 30 for the third successive season.

> **Almagro's form during 2009 enabled him to finish in the top 30 for the third successive season**

PHILIPP **KOHLSCHREIBER**

» DATE OF BIRTH: 16 October 1983 | **BORN:** Augsburg, Germany

Lives: Altstaetten, Switzerland

Height: 5'10" (178 cm)

Weight: 154 lbs (70 kg)

Style: Right-handed, one-handed backhand

Turned pro: 2001

Career singles titles: 2

ATP World Tour Masters 1000 titles: 0

Grand Slam titles: 0

Career-high South African Airways ATP Ranking: No.22 (Sep 09)

Career win-loss record: 148-134

Career prize money: $3,045,616

Career win-loss vs. top 10: 13-25

Barclays ATP World Tour Final titles: 0

South African Airways 2009 ATP Ranking: No.27

It was in 2004 that Philipp Kohlschreiber broke into the top 100 for the first time, but it was three years later when he really made his mark among the game's elite. The right-hander from Augsburg collected his first ATP World Tour title on home soil in Munich in 2007 when he beat Russia's Mikhail Youzhny in the final, and since then he has been a permanent fixture inside the top 40 of the last three year-end ATP world ranking lists.

Kohlschreiber's highlights during 2009 included a run to the fourth round of the French Open, his best result yet at Roland Garros, including a third round victory over the in-form Novak Djokovic. The Swiss-based star also reached the final in Metz, two semi-finals in Halle and Vienna, and helped his country to the final of ARAG ATP World Team Championship in Dusseldorf.

He also produced some great tennis wearing German colours when he notched up three impressive Davis Cup victories in the first round and quarter-finals against Austrian Jurgen Melzer and Spaniards Tommy Robredo and Fernando Verdasco. The German is also an accomplished doubles player with six titles to his name.

❝❝ The German's highlights in 2009 include helping his country reach the final of the ARAG ATP World Team Championship **❞❞**

©Christof Koepsel/Bongarts/Getty Images

©Jim McIsaac/Getty Images

JURGEN **MELZER**

» DATE OF BIRTH: 22 May 1981 | **BORN:** Vienna, Austria

STATISTICS

Lives: Vienna, Austria

Height: 6'0" (183 cm)

Weight: 178 lbs (81 kg)

Style: Left-handed, two-handed backhand

Turned pro: 1999

Career singles titles: 2

ATP World Tour Masters 1000 titles: 0

Grand Slam titles: 0

Career-high South African Airways ATP Ranking: No.26 (May 09)

Career win-loss record: 201-197

Career prize money: $3,751,352

Career win-loss vs. top 10: 6-36

Barclays ATP World Tour Final titles: 0

South African Airways 2009 ATP Ranking: No.28

This talented left-hander from Austria is an accomplished singles and doubles player who on his day can beat the best in the world.

Melzer has finished inside the top 100 of the South African Airways ATP rankings for the last eight years, and has claimed two singles titles, reached another six singles finals and won six doubles trophies since turning professional in 1999.

His first piece of singles silverware came on clay in Bucharest in 2006, but 2009 was his best season so far, a year in which he grabbed his second singles and fifth and sixth doubles titles.

The former Junior Wimbledon boys' singles champion made the semi-finals in Umag and in Bangkok, before ending his season on a high by becoming the first Austrian in 21 years to win the Vienna title when he beat top-seeded Croatian Marin Cilic in the final. Melzer also reached the Vienna doubles final with fellow countryman Julian Knowle, the man he has won four of his six titles with. His end-of-season form left Melzer with his best ever year-end ranking of No.28.

** Melzer is a former Junior Wimbledon champion who has collected two singles titles and six doubles trophies in his career **

VIKTOR **TROICKI**

» DATE OF BIRTH: 10 February 1986 | **BORN:** Belgrade, Serbia

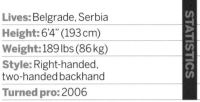

PLAYER **PROFILES**

STATISTICS

Lives: Belgrade, Serbia

Height: 6'4" (193 cm)

Weight: 189 lbs (86 kg)

Style: Right-handed, two-handed backhand

Turned pro: 2006

Career singles titles: 0

ATP World Tour Masters 1000 titles: 0

Grand Slam titles: 0

Career-high South African Airways ATP Ranking: No.24 (Aug 09)

Career win-loss record: 59-57

Career prize money: $1,355,987

Career win-loss vs. top 10: 3-17

Barclays ATP World Tour Final titles: 0

South African Airways 2009 ATP Ranking: No.29

This young Serb has enjoyed a steady rise up the rankings since turning professional in 2006, and has now firmly established himself among the best players in the world. In 2008 the Belgrade-born right-hander reached his first ATP World Tour final in Washington DC and appeared in another three quarter-finals in 's-Hertogenbosch, Tokyo and Moscow to end the year inside the top 100 for the first time in his career.

Troicki made even greater strides during 2009, however, rising 28 places between January and December to claim his first year-end top 30 listing. That came about thanks to another appearance in a final, this time in Bangkok where he beat Frenchman Jo-Wilfried Tsonga along the way. He also reached the semi-finals in Zagreb and made the third round at Wimbledon for the first time where he lost to Andy Murray. Another highlight during 2009 came in Dusseldorf where Troicki was part of the Serbian team that lifted the ARAG ATP World Team Championship title, winning three of his four singles matches during the week.

©Pornchai/AFP/Getty Images

❝ Troicki broke into the top 100 during 2008 and his form in 2009 enabled him to secure his first year-end top 30 listing ❞

©Lucas Dawson/Getty Images

© Jasper Juinen/Getty Images

JUAN **MONACO**

» DATE OF BIRTH: 29 March 1984 | **BORN:** Tandil, Argentina

Lives: Buenos Aires, Argentina	
Height: 6'1" (185 cm)	
Weight: 169 lbs (77 kg)	
Style: Right-handed, two-handed backhand	
Turned pro: 2002	
Career singles titles: 3	
ATP World Tour Masters 1000 titles: 0	
Grand Slam titles: 0	
Career-high South African Airways ATP Ranking: No.14 (Feb 08)	
Career win-loss record: 156-126	
Career prize money: $2,711,427	
Career win-loss vs. top 10: 7-25	
Barclays ATP World Tour Final titles: 0	
South African Airways 2009 ATP Ranking: No.30	

Juan Monaco is capable of beating anyone in the world on his day on a clay court and his record on the 'dirt' over the years proves it. Since turning professional back in 2002, the right-hander from Tandil – a hotbed of tennis talent since 2009 US Open champion Juan Martin Del Potro comes from the same town – has appeared in nine ATP World Tour clay court singles finals, winning three of them.

His first appearance in a final came in 2005 in Casablanca, but he improved on that in some style two years later when he enjoyed his best season to date, ending the year with three singles trophies.

He enjoyed a hat-trick of successes in Kitzbuhel, Poertschach and Buenos Aires in 2007, form that earned him a ranking leap of around 40 places between January and

December, from No.69 to what is so far his best year-end ranking of No.23.

In the last two seasons Monaco reached another five singles finals, including three in 2009 in Bucharest, Båstad and Buenos Aires. He is also a very capable doubles player who has already collected two titles. The South American also reached the semi-finals of the US Open in 2006 with fellow Argentine Maximo Gonzalez.

© Clive Brunskill/Getty Images

> **Monaco is a master on a clay court – the Argentine has reached nine singles finals on the surface, winning three of them**

©Julian Finney/Getty Images

Despite missing two months with a knee injury, Montanes still managed to win two singles titles in 2009

ALBERT **MONTANES**

» DATE OF BIRTH: 26 November 1980 | **BORN:** Sant Carles de la Rapita

STATISTICS

Lives: Barcelona, Spain	
Height: 5'9" (175 cm)	
Weight: 155 lbs (70 kg)	
Style: Right-handed, one-handed backhand	
Turned pro: 1999	
Career singles titles: 3	
ATP World Tour Masters 1000 titles: 0	
Grand Slam titles: 0	
Career-high South African Airways ATP Ranking: No.28 (May 09)	
Career win-loss record: 143-170	
Career prize money: $2,949,824	
Career win-loss vs. top 10: 3-19	
Barclays ATP World Tour Final titles: 0	
South African Airways 2009 ATP Ranking: No.31	

A nother self-confessed Spanish clay court specialist, Albert Montanes enjoyed a superb season in 2009, highlighted by the second and third ATP World Tour titles of his career and his highest ever year-end South African Airways ATP ranking of No.31. It took the Spaniard five attempts to win his first trophy after losing the first four finals of his career, but once he got his hands on his first piece of tour silverware in Amersfoort in 2008, his confidence seemed to grow and grow.

His achievements during 2009 are all the more remarkable given he was forced to miss two months of the season with a knee injury, but he still managed to win titles in Estoril, outlasting American James Blake in the championship decider, and later in the year in Bucharest where he beat Argentine Juan Monaco in the final.

During his week in Estoril, Montanes became the first player since South African Wes Moodie in October 2005 to win an ATP World Tour title having saved a match point in two different matches along the way.

He came back from the brink first against Frenchman Gilles Simon in the quarter-finals and repeated his escape act in the final when he saved two match points against Blake during the second set.

©Clive Brunskill/Getty Images

" The self-confessed movie addict produced a performance to remember in 2009 when he won his first singles title in Stuttgart **"**

JEREMY **CHARDY**

》 DATE OF BIRTH: 12 February 1987 | **BORN:** Pau, France

STATISTICS

Lives:	Boeil-Bezing, France
Height:	6'2" (188 cm)
Weight:	165 lbs (75 kg)
Style:	Right-handed, two-handed backhand
Turned pro:	2005
Career singles titles:	1
ATP World Tour Masters 1000 titles:	0
Grand Slam titles:	0
Career-high South African Airways ATP Ranking:	No.31 (Nov 2009)
Career win-loss record:	47-42
Career prize money:	$1,132,067
Career win-loss vs. top 10:	1-6
Barclays ATP World Tour Final titles:	0
South African Airways 2009 ATP Ranking:	No.32

This flamboyant Frenchman was one of the new faces making a real name for himself on the ATP World Tour in 2009 after he enjoyed a red hot run of form at the start of the season before claiming his first singles title in the summer.

The former Junior Wimbledon champion reached his maiden tour final at the SA Tennis Open in Johannesburg in February before an appearance in the semi-finals in Delray Beach, USA, a couple of weeks later. The man from the Pyrenees finally discovered what it feels like to be an ATP World Tour title winner when he beat Romanian Victor Hanescu in the Stuttgart final in July and his overall form during the season enabled him to record his first year-end South African Airways ATP ranking inside the top 50.

Many fans – particularly his French fans – will remember Chardy first hitting the headlines when he reached the fourth round at Roland Garros as the world No.145 in 2008, a run that included a five-set victory over world No.7 David Nalbandian, a victory he still considers his best-ever performance. And talking of performances, the self-confessed Hollywood addict says he would like to be an actor after hanging up his rackets.

PAUL-HENRI **MATHIEU**

» DATE OF BIRTH: 12 January 1982 | **BORN:** Strasbourg, France

STATISTICS

Lives: Geneva, Switzerland

Height: 6'1" (185 cm)

Weight: 163 lbs (74 kg)

Style: Right-handed, two-handed backhand

Turned pro: 1999

Career singles titles: 4

ATP World Tour Masters 1000 titles: 0

Grand Slam titles: 0

Career-high South African Airways ATP Ranking: No.12 (Apr 08)

Career win-loss record: 208-193

Career prize money: $3,809,279

Career win-loss vs. top 10: 10-43

Barclays ATP World Tour Final titles: 0

South African Airways 2009 ATP Ranking: No.33

" A runner-up finish in Hamburg and another two semi-final appearances helped him finish the year in the top 35 "

Paul-Henri Mathieu burst into the spotlight in 2002 when he produced one of his best seasons to date as a bright-eyed 20-year-old. The man from Strasbourg, in north-east France, attracted the attention of fans worldwide with his aggressive baseline game. At Roland Garros he reached the fourth round before letting slip a two-set lead over eventual champion Andre Agassi, he won the Moscow event as a qualifier and a week later became the first Frenchman to win back-to-back titles since Henri Leconte in 1986 when he claimed the Lyon trophy on home soil. His form during that season earned him the ATP Newcomer of the Year award and saw him climb more than 100 places in the rankings. He began 2002 at No.142 in the ATP South African Airways rankings and finished the year listed as the 36th best player in the world.

Since then the former French Open junior champion has added another two pieces of singles silverware to his trophy cabinet – both coming on his favoured clay and both in 2007 in Gstaad and Casablanca – and has appeared in another four finals.

One of those runner-up spots came at the ATP World Tour 500 event in Hamburg in July 2009, the best week of his season. The right-hander enjoyed victories over Viktor Troicki and Pablo Cuevas before falling to Russian Nikolay Davydenko in the final at the Rothenbaum Club. His year also featured semi-final finishes in Brisbane and Metz, results that helped him achieve a top-35 ranking for the third straight year.

JOHN **ISNER**

》 DATE OF BIRTH: 16 April 1985 | **BORN:** Greensboro, North Carolina, USA

STATISTICS

Lives: Tampa, Florida, USA

Height: 6'9" (206 cm)

Weight: 245 lbs (111 kg)

Style: Right-handed, two-handed backhand

Turned pro: 2007

Career singles titles: 0

ATP World Tour Masters 1000 titles: 0

Grand Slam titles: 0

Career-high South African Airways ATP Ranking: No.34 (Nov 09)

Career win-loss record: 46-42

Career prize money: $868,794

Career win-loss vs. top 10: 3-7

Barclays ATP World Tour Final titles: 0

South African Airways 2009 ATP Ranking: No.34

At 6ft 9" tall it's hardly surprising that John Isner considers his serve to be his biggest weapon, but he also has a solid all-round game that was put in place during his years playing college tennis at the University of Georgia from 2004-07. Isner excelled in the system, earning All-American honours every season and ended his days in Georgia as the university's all-time leader in singles and doubles wins.

Isner, who wears a size 15 shoe, didn't take long to make an impact on the ATP World Tour either, reaching 125 in the world rankings after just six months of playing tournaments, including a run to the final in Washington as a wild card in 2007 where he won five successive third-set tie-breaks.

He took his game to another level in 2009 when he racked up quarter-final finishes in Auckland, Houston, Los Angeles and Bangkok, semi-final runs in Indianapolis and Washington and made the fourth round of the US Open where he beat Andy Roddick in five sets. His form last season earned him his highest year-end ranking of No.34.

❝ In reaching the final in Washington DC in 2007, the 6ft 9" American won an incredible five successive third-set tie-breaks **❞**

> ❝ Andreev enjoyed another solid season in 2009 to finish inside the top 35 for the third successive season ❞

©Matthew Stockman/Getty Images

IGOR **ANDREEV**

» DATE OF BIRTH: 14 July 1983 | **BORN:** Moscow, Russia

Lives: Moscow, Russia

Height: 6'1" (185 cm)

Weight: 176 lbs (80 kg)

Style: Right-handed, two-handed backhand

Turned pro: 2002

Career singles titles: 3

ATP World Tour Masters 1000 titles: 0

Grand Slam titles: 0

Career-high South African Airways ATP Ranking: No.18 (Nov 08)

Career win-loss record: 191-166

Career prize money: $3,545,933

Career win-loss vs. top 10: 10-34

Barclays ATP World Tour Finals titles: 0

South African Airways 2009 ATP Ranking: No.35

The Russian has used his powerful baseline game to become one of the most dangerous players on clay on his day, a reputation that was reinforced when the Muscovite reached the quarterfinals of the 2007 French Open.

Andreev has three ATP World Tour singles titles to his name, all of which came during a purple patch in 2005 and, appropriately, it was in Valencia, the city he made his training base as a 15-year-old, where he won his first. During his run to the Spanish clay court title he became one of only two players in 2005 to beat Rafael Nadal on the 'dirt', before going on to collect trophies in Palermo and in his hometown of Moscow when he recovered from a set and 0-4 to outlast Germany's Nicolas Kiefer in the final.

In 2006 Andreev was sidelined when he was forced to undergo left knee surgery but showed his determination and dedication to his profession on his return by producing tennis that earned him the 2007 ATP Comeback Player of the Year award after climbing around 200 places in the rankings between April and December to finish just outside the top 30.

The 2008 season was another fine period for the Russian when he reached two finals in Umag and Gstaad, results that helped him peak at a career-best No.18 at the end of the year. His 2009 season featured three semi-finals – they came in Casablanca, Gstaad and New Haven – as well as a fourth round finish at Wimbledon to leave him as the Russian No.3 behind Nikolay Davydenko and Mikhail Youzhny with his third successive year-end ranking inside the top 35.

THOMAZ **BELLUCCI**

» DATE OF BIRTH: 30 December 1987 | BORN: Tiete, Brazil

STATISTICS

Lives: Sao Paulo, Brazil	
Height: 6'2" (188 cm)	
Weight: 177 lbs (80 kg)	
Style: Left-handed, two-handed backhand	
Turned pro: 2005	
Career singles titles: 1	
ATP World Tour Masters 1000 titles: 0	
Grand Slam titles: 0	
Career-high South African Airways ATP Ranking: No.36 (Nov 09)	
Career win-loss record: 25-34	
Career prize money: $672,807	
Career win-loss vs. top 10: 0-4	
Barclays ATP World Tour Finals titles: 0	
South African Airways 2009 ATP Ranking: No.36	

Thomaz Bellucci has enjoyed a steady rise up the South African Airways ATP rankings over the last five years since turning pro in 2005 and at the end of 2009 found himself at a career-high listing inside the top 40. The first signs that the left-hander was a world class player in the making came in 2008 when he won three successive clay court Challengers, a run of form that enabled him to end the season in the top 100 for the first time.

Since then, the self-confessed lover of clay has simply kept on rising. His first ATP World Tour singles final came in February 2009 when he finished second best to Spain's Tommy Robredo on home soil in Costa do Sauipe, before an even more impressive week in Gstaad in late July. He arrived at the Swiss clay court event as a qualifier, but rattled off seven victories over the likes of Stanislas Wawrinka, Nicolas Kiefer and Igor Andreev, to capture his maiden singles crown and become the first Brazilian since Ricardo Mello in 2004 to win an ATP World Tour singles title.

Bellucci finished 2009 with a flourish, qualifying for the ATP World Tour Masters 1000 in Shanghai before a semi-final finish on hard in Stockholm and his second Challenger title of the year in Sao Paulo. As a result, the South American ended the season with a career-best ranking of No.36 – the first Brazilian to finish in the top 50 since former world No.1 and triple French Open champion Gustavo Kuerten in 2004.

❝ The Brazilian won his first singles title in Gstaad in July 2009, beating Wawrinka, Kiefer and Andreev along the way ❞

© J Hannah Johnston/Getty Images

© Junko Kimura/Getty Images

IVO **KARLOVIC**

» **DATE OF BIRTH:** 28 February 1979 | **BORN:** Zagreb, Croatia

STATISTICS

Lives: Zagreb, Croatia
Height: 6'10" (208 cm)
Weight: 230 lbs (104 kg)
Style: Right-handed, one-handed backhand
Turned pro: 2000
Career singles titles: 4
ATP World Tour Masters 1000 titles: 0
Grand Slam titles: 0
Career-high South African Airways ATP Ranking: No.14 (Aug 08)
Career win-loss record: 161-150
Career prize money: $3,331,074
Career win-loss vs. top 10: 12-29
Barclays ATP World Tour Finals titles: 0
South African Airways 2009 ATP Ranking: No.37

A t 6ft 10", Ivo Karlovic is the tallest player ever to feature inside the top 100 of the South African Airways ATP rankings and his extraordinary height has helped him notch up numerous records since turning professional in 2000. He first burst onto the scene when he shocked defending champion Lleyton Hewitt in the first round at Wimbledon in 2003 – his first ever Grand Slam victory – and has been tormenting opponents with his ferocious serve ever since.

His best year so far came in 2007 when he won three titles on three different surfaces – Houston, Nottingham and Stockholm – and reached the final in San Jose. A year later he peaked at a career-high ranking of No.18 during a season which included his fourth singles trophy when he defended his Nottingham title.

Karlovic produced another solid season in 2009 when he reached the semi-finals in Belgrade on clay and three successive quarter-finals at Queen's, Wimbledon and Washington DC. His run to the last eight at Wimbledon included victories over top ten players Jo-Wilfried Tsonga and Fernando Verdasco and an incredible run of serving that saw him hit 208 aces and hold serve for 105 successive games.

As well as delivering a record-breaking 77 aces during a five-hour, 59-minute epic with Radek Stepanek in the Davis Cup semi-finals in September, Karlovic also led the 2009 Ricoh ATP MatchFacts in aces struck (890), service games won (92%) and first serve points won (85%).

❝ His run to the last eight at Wimbledon in 2009 saw him hit 208 aces and hold serve for 105 games ❞

©Nick Laham/Getty Images

JANKO **TIPSAREVIC**

» **DATE OF BIRTH:** 22 June 1984 | **BORN:** Belgrade, Serbia

Lives: Belgrade, Serbia

Height: 5'11" (180 cm)

Weight: 176 lbs (80 kg)

Style: Right-handed, two-handed backhand

Turned pro: 2002

Career singles titles: 0

ATP World Tour Masters 1000 titles: 0

Grand Slam titles: 0

Career-high South African Airways ATP Ranking: No.33 (May 08)

Career win-loss record: 109-115

Career prize money: $2,239,855

Career win-loss vs. top 10: 6-20

Barclays ATP World Tour Finals titles: 0

South African Airways 2009 ATP Ranking: No.38

> ❝ Tipsarevic reached his first ATP World Tour final in 2009 and also helped Serbia win the ARAG ATP Word Team Championship ❞

© John Thys/Getty Images

This popular right-hander from Belgrade has managed to improve his year-end ranking season-on-season over the past four years and his tennis during 2009 suggests his wait for a first ATP World Tour title won't go on for much longer.

Tipsarevic, who is well known for his love of classic literature and has a tattoo on his left arm with the Dostoyevski quotation 'Beauty will save the world', ended 2009 at No.38 in the South African Airways ATP rankings – his highest ever season-ending listing and just five places below his best-ever ranking which came in May 2008.

Tipsarevic, who won the Australian Open boys' singles and was once the junior world No.2, enjoyed a consistent 2009 when he reached three quarter-finals, one semi-final and his first ATP World Tour singles final on indoor hard courts in Moscow. His quarter-final appearances were spread over the season, in Chennai in January, Eastbourne in June and in September in the French city of Metz.

He went one better in Vienna during the European indoor swing, but saved the best week of his career until Moscow where he narrowly lost to local favourite Mikhail Youzhny in the final. Tipsarevic also had a good year in team tennis too when he helped Serbia win the ARAG ATP World Team Championship in Dusseldorf in May. The Belgrade-born star ended the week with a 100% singles record, beating Philipp Kohlschreiber in straight sets to clinch a 2-1 victory for the Serbs over hosts Germany in the final.

ANDREAS **BECK**

Lives: Ravensburg, Germany

Height: 6'3" (190 cm)

Weight: 198 lbs (90 kg)

Style: Left-handed, two-handed backhand

Turned pro: 2003

Career singles titles: 0

ATP World Tour Masters 1000 titles: 0

Grand Slam titles: 0

Career-high South African Airways ATP Ranking: No.33 (Nov 08)

Career win-loss record: 29-34

Career prize money: $767,130

Career win-loss vs. top 10: 1-5

Barclays ATP World Tour Finals titles: 0

South African Airways 2009 ATP Ranking: No.39

A fter four years working his way up the South African Airways ATP rankings thanks to success on the ITF Futures tour, this left-hander from Germany made his breakthrough during 2008 when he rose nearly 100 places to end the season just outside the top 100. During 2008 Beck won two Challenger Tour titles, reached another two finals, fought his way through qualifying at Wimbledon and at the US Open where he also won a round and made his first ATP World Tour quarter-final on grass in Halle.

The 6ft 3" youngster enjoyed even greater success on the road during 2009, however, appearing in his first singles and doubles finals, and breaking into the top 100 for the first time in February. His first notable result

of the season came at the Australian Open where he qualified and won a round, and it was in Monte Carlo where he next stole the limelight, qualifying and beating Nicolas Kiefer, Gilles Simon and Juan Monaco in the main draw to reach the last eight of the clay court ATP World Tour Masters 1000.

In July he appeared in his first singles final where he lost to Brazilian Thomaz Bellucci, and a doubles final in Halle with Swiss Marco Chiudinelli, before reaching back-to-back quarter-finals in Metz and Bangkok and winning a round at the Rakuten Japan Open in Tokyo and at the ATP World Tour Masters 1000 Shanghai. His end-of-season form saw him peak at a career-best No.33 in November and finish the year inside the top 50 at No.39 for the first time in his career.

> **Beck turned heads with his tennis at the ATP World Tour Masters 1000 in Monte Carlo, beating Kiefer, Simon and Monaco**

©Alexander Hassenstein/Bongarts/Getty Images

©Kiyoshi Ota/Getty Images

BENJAMIN **BECKER**

» **DATE OF BIRTH:** 16 June 1981 | **BORN:** Merzig, Germany

STATISTICS

Lives: Fort Lauderdale, FL, USA	
Height: 5'10" (178 cm)	
Weight: 174 lbs (79 kg)	
Style: Right-handed, two-handed backhand	
Turned Pro: 2005	
Career singles titles: 1	
ATP World Tour Masters 1000 titles: 0	
Grand Slam titles: 0	
Career-high South African Airways ATP Ranking: No.38 (May 07)	
Career win-loss record: 55-79	
Career prize money: $1,342,968	
Career win-loss vs. top 10: 3-14	
Barclays ATP World Tour Finals titles: 0	
South African Airways 2009 ATP Ranking: No.40	

Despite his world famous tennis surname, Benjamin, or Benni as he's known on tour, is no relation to the former world No.1 and six-time Grand Slam champion Boris. Having spent four successful years in the US collegiate system at Baylor University in Texas, Becker first made a name for himself by beating Andre Agassi in the American's last match as a professional at the 2006 US Open. The right-hander enjoyed a fantastic run at Flushing Meadows that year, rattling off victories over Filippo Volandri, Sebastien Grosjean and Agassi before finally losing to Andy Roddick in the last 16.

Twelve months later the German reached his first ATP World Tour final in Bangkok, but 2009 was arguably his best period yet as he ended the season with a career-high end-of-year ranking and his first piece of ATP silverware. During the first five months of 2009 Becker compiled a 27-4 Challenger Tour record, including four titles, before qualifying for and winning the Ordina Open in 's-Hertogenbosch, where he beat top seed Fernando Verdasco in the second round and Dutchman Raemon Sluiter in the final.

His form saw him jump from No.135 at the beginning of 2009 to No.40 by season-end, just two places off his best ever ranking of No.38 which came in 2007. Becker also reached his first doubles final with Frank Moser in Los Angeles during the summer of 2009.

❝ 2009 was a year to remember for the German – his first title at the Ordina Open and a ranking jump of nearly 100 places ❞

BOB **BRYAN** & MIKE **BRYAN**

" The Americans have been crowned ATP World Tour Doubles Champions five times **"**

©Clive Brunskill/Getty Images

» BOB BRYAN (USA)

Date of birth:	29 April 1978
Born:	Camarillo, California, USA
Lives:	Wesley Chapel, Florida, USA
Height:	6'4" (193 cm)
Weight:	202 lbs (92 kg)
Style:	Left-handed, one-handed backhand
Turned pro:	1998
Career doubles titles:	56
ATP World Tour Masters 1000 doubles titles:	13
Grand Slam doubles titles:	7
Career-high ATP Doubles Ranking:	No.1 (Sep 03)
Career win-loss doubles record:	590-208
Career prize money:	$6,360,098
Barclays ATP World Tour Finals titles:	3
2009 ATP Doubles Ranking:	No.1

» MIKE BRYAN (USA)

Date of birth:	29 April 1978
Born:	Camarillo, California, USA
Lives:	Wesley Chapel, Florida, USA
Height:	6'3" (190 cm)
Weight:	192 lbs (87 kg)
Style:	Right-handed, one-handed backhand
Turned pro:	1998
Career doubles titles:	58
ATP World Tour Masters 1000 doubles titles:	13
Grand Slam doubles titles:	7
Career-high ATP Doubles Ranking:	No.1 (Sep 03)
Career win-loss doubles record:	604-210
Career prize money:	$6,131,175
Barclays ATP World Tour Finals titles:	3
2009 ATP Doubles Ranking:	No.1

The American twins from California are one of the most exciting doubles teams around and have enjoyed huge success on the ATP World Tour, at Grand Slam level and representing their country in the Davis Cup. The brothers have collected seven Grand Slam doubles crowns, won the Barclays ATP World Tour Finals three times, have been crowned ATP World Tour Doubles Champions five times, and own the best ever doubles record in US Davis Cup history (won 16, lost two). Add to that another eight Grand Slam mixed doubles titles between them and now even a successful music career (The Bryan Bros. Band features Bob on keyboards and Mike on drums and guitar and released an EP in September 2009) and you can see why the duo rock the doubles world on and off court.

> The duo picked up nine titles in 2009 including five ATP World Tour Masters 1000s

©Cameron Spencer/Getty Images

(L-R) DANIEL NESTOR & NENAD ZIMONJIC

DANIEL NESTOR & NENAD ZIMONJIC

» Daniel Nestor (CAN)

Date of birth: 4 September 1972
Born: Belgrade, Yugoslavia
Lives: Toronto, Canada/Nassau, The Bahamas
Height: 6'3" (190 cm)
Weight: 190 lbs (86 kg)
Style: Left-handed, two-handed backhand
Turned pro: 1991
Career doubles titles: 64
ATP World Tour Masters 1000 doubles titles: 13
Grand Slam doubles titles: 5
Career-high ATP Doubles Ranking: No.1 (Aug 02)
Career win-loss doubles record: 723-280
Career prize money: $8,235,323
Barclays ATP World Tour Finals titles: 2
2009 ATP Doubles Ranking: No.3

» Nenad Zimonjic (SRB)

Date of birth: 4 June 1976
Born: Belgrade, Serbia
Lives: Belgrade, Serbia
Height: 6'3" (190 cm)
Weight: 200 lbs (91 kg)
Style: Right-handed, one-handed backhand
Turned pro: 1995
Career doubles titles: 32
ATP World Tour Masters 1000 doubles titles: 9
Grand Slam doubles titles: 2
Career-high ATP Doubles Ranking: No.1 (Nov 08)
Career win-loss doubles record: 398-212
Career prize money: $4,277,268
Barclays ATP World Tour Finals titles: 1
2009 ATP Doubles Ranking: No.3

STATISTICS

Considering both became new dads towards the end of 2008, their performance over the next 12 months was nothing short of remarkable. They teamed up to win nine titles during 2009 – including five ATP World Tour Masters 1000s in Monte-Carlo, Rome, Madrid, Cincinnati and Paris – but their most impressive achievement was the defence of the Wimbledon doubles title they won in 2008. The duo have seven Grand Slam doubles titles between them, both have been ranked No.1 in the world, and both have won the season-ending Barclays ATP World Tour Finals during their careers. Having been dislodged from top spot in the ATP Doubles Team Rankings by the Bryans right at the end of 2009, Nestor and Zimonjic will be aiming for yet more of the biggest titles during 2010.

LUKAS **DLOUHY** & LEANDER **PAES**

(L-R) LEANDER PAES & LUKAS DLOUHY

" The pair won two Grand Slams in 2009 and finished the year as the fourth-best team in the world "

©Clive Brunskill/Getty Images

》 **Lukas Dlouhy** (CZE)

Date of birth: 9 April 1983	
Born: Pisek, Czech Republic	
Lives: Monte Carlo, Monaco	
Height: 6'1" (185 cm)	
Weight: 194 lbs (88 kg)	
Style: Right-handed, two-handed backhand	
Turned pro: 2001	
Career doubles titles: 7	
ATP World Tour Masters 1000 doubles titles: 0	
Grand Slam doubles titles: 2	
Career-high ATP Doubles Ranking: No.5 (Jun 09)	
Career win-loss doubles record: 128-83	
Career prize money: $2,246,182	
Barclays ATP World Tour Finals titles: 0	
2009 ATP Doubles Ranking: No.6	

》 **Leander Paes** (IND)

Date of birth: 17 June 1973	
Born: Calcutta, India	
Lives: Calcutta, India/Orlando, FL, USA	
Height: 5'10" (178 cm)	
Weight: 171 lbs (78 kg)	
Style: Right-handed, one-handed backhand	
Turned pro: 1991	
Career doubles titles: 42	
ATP World Tour Masters 1000 doubles titles: 7	
Grand Slam doubles titles: 6	
Career-high ATP Doubles Ranking: No.1 (Jun 99)	
Career win-loss doubles record: 524-275	
Career prize money: $5,506,550	
Barclays ATP World Tour Finals titles: 0	
2009 ATP Doubles Ranking: No.8	

STATISTICS

This Czech-Indian team got together midway through the 2008 season and enjoyed huge success on court during 2009, arguably establishing themselves as the most successful team in the world at the biggest events. Some might say that two titles is less than outstanding, but those two titles were both Grand Slams, the pair triumphing on clay at Roland Garros in June and three months later at the US Open. In addition, they also reached the 2009 Australian Open semi-finals and the final of the Rotterdam ATP World Tour 500, results that helped them finish the year as the fourth-best pair in the world. Paes' story is remarkable considering he was sidelined in 2003 after being struck down with a suspected brain tumour, later diagnosed as a parasitic infection of the brain.

DOUBLES

(L-R) MARIUSZ FYRSTENBERG
& MARCIN MATKOWSKI

> Two titles in 2009 meant the Poles qualified for the Barclays ATP World Tour Finals

© Julian Finney/Getty Images

MARIUSZ **FYRSTENBERG**
& MARCIN **MATKOWSKI**

›› Mariusz Fyrstenberg (POL)

Date of birth: 8 July 1980
Born: Warsaw, Poland
Lives: Warsaw, Poland
Height: 6'4" (193 cm)
Weight: 176 lbs (80 kg)
Style: Left-handed, two-handed backhand
Turned pro: 2001
Career doubles titles: 10
ATP World Tour Masters 1000 doubles titles: 1
Grand Slam doubles titles: 0
Career-high ATP Doubles Ranking: No.11 (Feb 09)
Career win-loss doubles record: 205-155
Career prize money: $1,216,684
Barclays ATP World Tour Finals titles: 0
2009 ATP Doubles Ranking: No.18

›› Marcin Matkowski (POL)

Date of birth: 15 January 1981
Born: Barlinek, Poland
Lives: Szczecin, Poland
Height: 6'2" (188 cm)
Weight: 178 lbs (81 kg)
Style: Right-handed, two-handed backhand
Turned pro: 2003
Career doubles titles: 10
ATP World Tour Masters 1000 doubles titles: 1
Grand Slam doubles titles: 0
Career-high ATP Doubles Ranking: No.11 (Feb 09)
Career win-loss doubles record: 200-158
Career prize money: $1,207,349
Barclays ATP World Tour Finals titles: 0
2009 ATP Doubles Ranking: No.17

STATISTICS

After a less than perfect start to their friendship when they had an argument over a vacant seat at a junior training camp, this Polish pair have gone from strength to strength. Once Marcin Matkowski had graduated from UCLA, they teamed up to win their first ever professional event together – a Challenger in Matkowski's hometown, Szczecin, in 2001 – and since then have notched up ten doubles titles on the ATP World Tour, including one ATP World Tour Masters 1000 shield in Madrid in 2008. The duo collected two trophies in 2009 – on grass in Eastbourne and on indoor hard in Kuala Lumpur – and their form over the year meant they qualified for the end-of-season Barclays ATP World Tour Finals in London for the third time in their careers.

FRANTISEK **CERMAK** &
MICHAL **MERTINAK**

> **❝** They claimed five doubles titles during 2009 and reached the semi-finals at the Barclays ATP World Tour Finals **❞**

(L-R) FRANTISEK CERMAK & MICHAL MERTINAK

©Christopher Lee/Getty Images

❯❯ **Frantisek Cermak** (CZE)

Date of birth: 14 November 1976
Born: Valtice, Czech Republic
Lives: Kostice, Czech Republic
Height: 6'4" (193 cm)
Weight: 176 lbs (80 kg)
Style: Right-handed, two-handed backhand
Turned pro: 1998
Career doubles titles: 21
ATP World Tour Masters 1000 doubles titles: 0
Grand Slam doubles titles: 0
Career-high ATP Doubles Ranking: No.16 (Nov 09)
Career win-loss doubles record: 259-188
Career prize money: $1,453,177
Barclays ATP World Tour Finals titles: 0
2009 ATP Doubles Ranking: No.16

❯❯ **Michal Mertinak** (SVK)

Date of birth: 11 October 1979
Born: Povazska Bystrica, Slovak Republic
Lives: Bratislava, Slovak Republic
Height: 5'11" (180 cm)
Weight: 187 lbs (85 kg)
Style: Right-handed, two-handed backhand
Turned pro: 1999
Career doubles titles: 11
ATP World Tour Masters 1000 doubles titles: 0
Grand Slam doubles titles: 0
Career-high ATP Doubles Ranking: No.14 (Nov 09)
Career win-loss doubles record: 112-79
Career prize money: $950,690
Barclays ATP World Tour Finals titles: 0
2009 ATP Doubles Ranking: No.14

STATISTICS

T his Czech-Slovak doubles team decided to get together for the first time at the beginning of 2009 and haven't looked back since. Both had picked up ATP World Tour titles with other players before they gave their new partnership a go, and their success together last season has established them as one of the best pairs in the world. The duo teamed up to claim silverware in Acapulco, Stuttgart, Umag, Bucharest and Valencia, form that earned them one of eight qualification places at the end-of-season Barclays ATP World Tour Finals for the first time in their careers. Once in London, they produced some of their best tennis to reach the semi-finals. Both men ended the year with career-best ATP Doubles Rankings and went into the off season as the sixth best pair in the world.

(L-R) LUKASZ KUBOT & OLIVER MARACH

> **The duo had a memorable season – three titles, one runner-up finish and another seven semi-finals**

©Glyn Kirk/AFP/Getty Images

LUKASZ **KUBOT** &
OLIVER **MARACH**

STATISTICS

» **Lukasz Kubot** (POL)

Date of birth: 16 May 1982
Born: Boleslawiec, Poland
Lives: Lubin, Poland
Height: 6'3" (190 cm)
Weight: 190 lbs (86 kg)
Style: Right-handed, two-handed backhand
Turned pro: 2002
Career doubles titles: 3
ATP World Tour Masters 1000 doubles titles: 0
Grand Slam doubles titles: 0
Career-high ATP Doubles Ranking: No.11 (Nov 09)
Career win-loss doubles record: 73-48
Career prize money: $1,077,689
Barclays ATP World Tour Finals titles: 0
2009 ATP Doubles Ranking: No.12

» **Oliver Marach** (AUT)

Date of birth: 16 July 1980
Born: Graz, Austria
Lives: Graz, Austria
Height: 6'1" (185 cm)
Weight: 172 lbs (78 kg)
Style: Right-handed, two-handed backhand
Turned pro: 1998
Career doubles titles: 5
ATP World Tour Masters 1000 doubles titles: 0
Grand Slam doubles titles: 0
Career-high ATP Doubles Ranking: No.12 (Nov 09)
Career win-loss doubles record: 91-70
Career prize money: $1,069,852
Barclays ATP World Tour Finals titles: 0
2009 ATP Doubles Ranking: No.13

This Austrian-Polish team enjoyed a truly memorable year during 2009, one that Lukasz Kubot, in particular, will remember for some time. As well as picking up three doubles titles – two on clay in Casablanca and Belgrade, and later in the year indoors in Vienna – the pair also qualified for the Barclays ATP World Tour Finals in London for the first time in their careers. In addition, they finished runners-up in Acapulco and made seven semi-finals including at the Australian Open. Kubot also had a great year on the singles court too. The Pole reached his first singles final as a lucky loser in Belgrade and beat Andy Roddick in Beijing, results that enabled him to end the year just outside the top 100 of the South African Airways ATP singles rankings.

MICHAEL **LLODRA** &
ANDY **RAM**

MICHAEL LLODRA

ANDY RAM

» **Michael Llodra** (FRA)

Date of birth: 18 May 1980

Born: Paris, France

Lives: Rueil Malmaison, France

Height: 6'3" (190 cm)

Weight: 176 lbs (80 kg)

Style: Left-handed, one-handed backhand

Turned pro: 1999

Career doubles titles: 17

ATP World Tour Masters 1000 doubles titles: 2

Grand Slam doubles titles: 3

Career-high ATP Doubles Ranking: No.8 (Jun 04)

Career win-loss doubles record: 247-156

Career prize money: $4,727,298

Barclays ATP World Tour Finals titles: 1

2009 ATP Doubles Ranking: No.49

» **Andy Ram** (ISR)

Date of birth: 10 April 1980

Born: Montevideo, Uruguay

Lives: Jerusalem, Israel

Height: 5'11" (180 cm)

Weight: 182 lbs (83 kg)

Style: Right-handed, one-handed backhand

Turned pro: 1998

Career doubles titles: 16

ATP World Tour Masters 1000 doubles titles: 3

Grand Slam doubles titles: 1

Career-high ATP Doubles Ranking: No.5 (Jul 08)

Career win-loss doubles record: 245-158

Career prize money: $2,150,142

Barclays ATP World Tour Finals titles: 0

2009 ATP Doubles Ranking: No.9

T wo of the most talented doubles players around, Israel's Andy Ram and Frenchman Michael Llodra, team up in 2010 with the aim of winning the biggest titles on the ATP World Tour. Both have tasted success at the highest level before with four Grand Slam doubles titles and 33 ATP World Tour doubles trophies between them. Ram made his name alongside fellow-Israeli Jonathan Erlich, but it was with Belarussian Max Mirnyi that he enjoyed success with in 2009, finishing as runners-up at the Barclays ATP World Tour Finals. Llodra is still very much a force on the singles court (he reached two finals in 2009 in Marseille and Lyon) but has also proved himself as a first-class doubles player having won three Grand Slams and a Barclays ATP World Tour Finals title alongside Fabrice Santoro in 2005.

©Xxxxx/Getty Images

DOUBLES

(L-R) MAHESH BHUPATHI & MAX MIRNYI

"This pair have won seven titles together, including the 2002 US Open"

©Mike Hewitt/Getty Images

MAHESH **BHUPATHI** &
MAX **MIRNYI**

STATISTICS

» **Mahesh Bhupathi** (IND)

Date of birth: 7 June 1974

Born: Madras, India

Lives: Bangalore, India

Height: 6'1" (185 cm)

Weight: 195 lbs (88 kg)

Style: Right-handed, two-handed backhand

Turned pro: 1995

Career doubles titles: 45

ATP World Tour Masters 1000 doubles titles: 12

Grand Slam doubles titles: 4

Career-high ATP Doubles Ranking: No.1 (Apr 99)

Career win-loss doubles record: 561-276

Career prize money: $4,977,447

Barclays ATP World Tour Finals titles: 0

2009 ATP Doubles Ranking: No.7

» **Max Mirnyi** (BLR)

Date of birth: 6 July 1977

Born: Minsk, Belarus

Lives: Bradenton, Florida, USA

Height: 6'5" (196 cm)

Weight: 205 lbs (93 kg)

Style: Right-handed, one-handed backhand

Turned pro: 1996

Career doubles titles: 36

ATP World Tour Masters 1000 doubles titles: 15

Grand Slam doubles titles: 4

Career-high ATP Doubles Ranking: No.1 (Jun 03)

Career win-loss doubles record: 477-238

Career prize money: $8,486,716

Barclays ATP World Tour Finals titles: 1

2009 ATP Doubles Ranking: No.11

Belarussian giant, Max 'The Beast' Mirnyi, and India's Mahesh Bhupathi will re-unite as a team during the 2010 ATP World Tour season and both men should have good memories of their last prolonged spell together. Although both have enjoyed great success with other partners (Mirnyi won two Grand Slams and the 2006 Barclays ATP World Tour Finals with Sweden's Jonas Bjorkman while Bhupathi claimed three majors with fellow Indian Leander Paes), they also have a fabulous record together having won seven doubles titles over the years, five of which came during a brilliant spell in 2003, and their biggest a year earlier when they won the US Open. If they can rediscover that same form they are sure to be competing for the biggest titles throughout 2010.

CALENDAR

2010 ATP WORLD TOUR

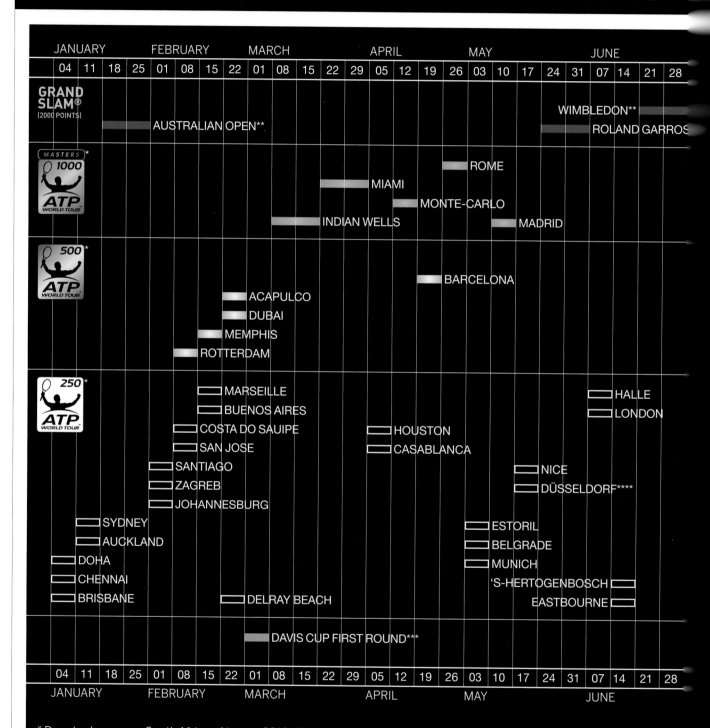

	JANUARY				FEBRUARY				MARCH				APRIL				MAY				JUNE			
	04	11	18	25	01	08	15	22	01	08	15	22	29	05	12	19	26	03	10	17	24	31	07	14	21	28

GRAND SLAM® (2000 POINTS)
- AUSTRALIAN OPEN**
- WIMBLEDON**
- ROLAND GARROS

MASTERS 1000 ATP WORLD TOUR *
- ROME
- MIAMI
- MONTE-CARLO
- INDIAN WELLS
- MADRID

500 ATP WORLD TOUR *
- BARCELONA
- ACAPULCO
- DUBAI
- MEMPHIS
- ROTTERDAM

250 ATP WORLD TOUR *
- MARSEILLE
- BUENOS AIRES
- COSTA DO SAUIPE
- SAN JOSE
- SANTIAGO
- ZAGREB
- JOHANNESBURG
- SYDNEY
- AUCKLAND
- DOHA
- CHENNAI
- BRISBANE
- DELRAY BEACH
- HOUSTON
- CASABLANCA
- NICE
- DÜSSELDORF****
- ESTORIL
- BELGRADE
- MUNICH
- 'S-HERTOGENBOSCH
- EASTBOURNE
- HALLE
- LONDON

DAVIS CUP FIRST ROUND***

	04	11	18	25	01	08	15	22	01	08	15	22	29	05	12	19	26	03	10	17	24	31	07	14	21	28
	JANUARY				FEBRUARY				MARCH				APRIL				MAY				JUNE			

* Denotes how many South African Airways 2010 ATP Rankings points are awarded to the winner.

** Grand Slams are not ATP events.

*** The Davis Cup is not an ATP event. It awards up to 625 South African Airways 2010 ATP Rankings points.

**** ARAG ATP World Team Championship

SEASON

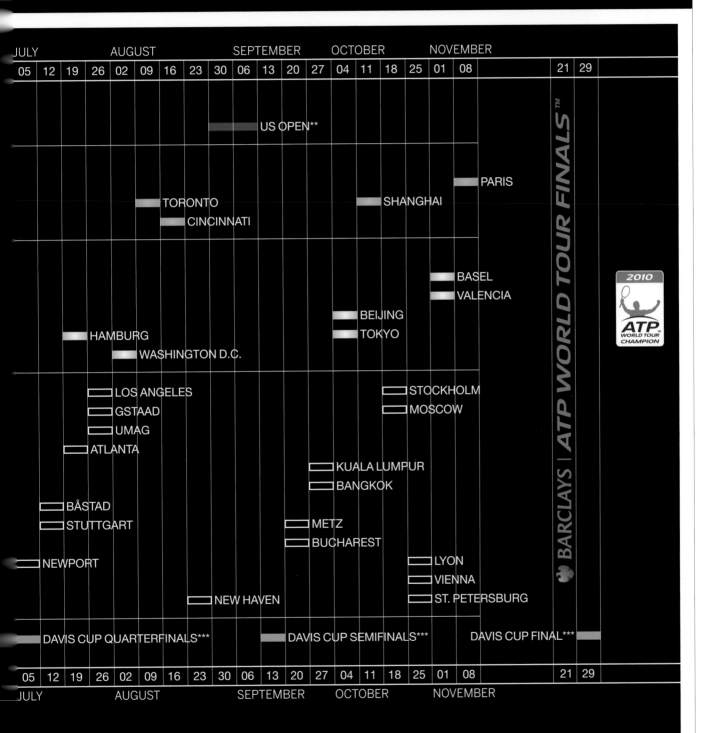

	JULY				AUGUST				SEPTEMBER			OCTOBER				NOVEMBER					
05	12	19	26	02	09	16	23	30	06	13	20	27	04	11	18	25	01	08		21	29

US OPEN**

PARIS

TORONTO
CINCINNATI

SHANGHAI

BASEL
VALENCIA

BEIJING
TOKYO

HAMBURG
WASHINGTON D.C.

LOS ANGELES
GSTAAD
UMAG
ATLANTA

STOCKHOLM
MOSCOW

KUALA LUMPUR
BANGKOK

BÅSTAD
STUTTGART

METZ
BUCHAREST

NEWPORT

LYON
VIENNA
ST. PETERSBURG

NEW HAVEN

BARCLAYS | ATP WORLD TOUR FINALS™

2010
ATP WORLD TOUR CHAMPION

DAVIS CUP QUARTERFINALS***   DAVIS CUP SEMIFINALS***   DAVIS CUP FINAL***

05	12	19	26	02	09	16	23	30	06	13	20	27	04	11	18	25	01	08		21	29
JULY				AUGUST					SEPTEMBER			OCTOBER					NOVEMBER				

JANUARY 4-9 | DOHA, QATAR

QATAR
EXXONMOBIL OPEN

TOURNAMENT WEBSITE:
www.qatartennis.org

Draw: Singles-32 Doubles-16
Prize money: $1,024,000
Surface: Hard
Venue: Khalifa Tennis Complex
Tournament director: Karim Alami
First held: 1993

The Doha event is one of the strongest ATP World Tour 250s on the calendar as the best players in the world kick-start their seasons eager to quickly find their best form with the Australian Open around the corner. In 2009 Briton Andy Murray made sure he had a very happy new year as he beat Andy Roddick in the final to defend the title he had won 12 months earlier. Qatar's tennis fans have seen some of the game's biggest stars performing at the Khalifa International Tennis Complex since the event began back in 1993. Fifteen-time Grand Slam champion Roger Federer has been a regular visitor, winning the title in 2005 and 2006, and former world No.1s Stefan Edberg from Sweden and Germany's Boris Becker both held the trophy aloft in the early 1990s.

PAST **CHAMPIONS**

YEAR	SINGLES	DOUBLES
2009	Andy Murray (GBR)	Marc Lopez (ESP) & Rafael Nadal (ESP)
2008	Andy Murray (GBR)	Philipp Kohlschreiber (GER) & David Skoch (CZE)
2007	Ivan Ljubicic (CRO)	Mikhail Youzhny (RUS) & Nenad Zimonjic (SRB)
2006	Roger Federer (SUI)	Jonas Bjorkman (SWE) & Max Mirnyi (BLR)
2005	Roger Federer (SUI)	Albert Costa (ESP) & Rafael Nadal (ESP)

JANUARY 4-10 | CHENNAI, CHINA

AIRCEL
CHENNAI OPEN

TOURNAMENT WEBSITE:
www.aircelchennaiopen.org

Draw: Singles-32 Doubles-16
Prize money: $398,250
Surface: Hard
Venue: SDAT Tennis Stadium
Tournament director: Fernando Soler
First held: 1996

Indian wild card Somdev Devvarman hit the headlines at the 2009 staging of the event as he reached his first ATP World Tour singles final. Ranked a modest world No.202 at the time, the local favourite beat the two-time former champion from Spain, Carlos Moya, and big-serving Croatian Ivo Karlovic along the way, but it was another star from Croatia, Marin Cilic, who stole the show in the final. Cilic began his year perfectly, at the same time giving India's tennis fans a glimpse of the kind of form he would reproduce throughout the entire season as he established himself firmly inside the top 20 by November. The Aircel Chennai Open roll of honour includes two former Grand Slam champions – Moya (2004 and 2005) and Australian Pat Rafter, who won the event in 1998.

MARIN CILIC

PAST **CHAMPIONS**

YEAR	SINGLES	DOUBLES
2009	Marin Cilic (CRO)	Eric Butorac (USA) & Rajeev Ram (USA)
2008	Mikhail Youzhny (RUS)	Sanchai Ratiwatana (THA) & Sonchat Ratiwatana (THA)
2007	Xavier Malisse (BEL)	Xavier Malisse (BEL) & Dick Norman (BEL)
2006	Ivan Ljubicic (CRO)	Michal Mertinak (CZE) & Petr Pala (CZE)
2005	Carlos Moya (ESP)	Yen-Hsun Lu (TPE) & Rainer Schuettler (GER)

ATP WORLD TOUR 250

JANUARY 3-10 | BRISBANE, AUSTRALIA

BRISBANE INTERNATIONAL

Sony Ericsson
WTA TOUR

TOURNAMENT WEBSITE:
www.brisbaneinternational.com.au

Draw: Singles-32 Doubles-16
Prize money: $372,500
Surface: Hard
Venue: Queensland Tennis Centre
Tournament director: Stephen Ayles
First held: 1956 (Adelaide from 1958-2008)

RADEK STEPANEK

BRISBANE

I n 2009 world class international tennis returned to Brisbane for the first time since 1994 and the stars assembled didn't disappoint. The top seed from Serbia, former Grand Slam champion Novak Djokovic, lost early, and it was the Czech Republic's Radek Stepanek who showed the young guns a thing or two, capturing the title at 30 years of age when he beat the in-form Spaniard Fernando Verdasco in the final. The 2010 line-up promises to be just as strong, headlined by former world No.1 Andy Roddick who will be joined by the likes of defending champion Stepanek, Tomas Berdych, Gael Monfils, Richard Gasquet, James Blake and Marcos Baghdatis. The Brisbane tournament is a combined event, also showcasing the best women in the world in a Sony Ericsson WTA Tour International draw.

PAST CHAMPIONS

YEAR	SINGLES	DOUBLES
2009	Radek Stepanek (CZE)	Marc Gicquel (FRA) & Jo-Wilfried Tsonga (FRA)
2008	Michael Llodra (FRA)	Martin Garcia (ARG) & Marcelo Melo (BRA)
2007	Novak Djokovic (SRB)	Wesley Moodie (RSA) & Todd Perry (AUS)
2006	Florent Serra (FRA)	Jonathan Erlich (ISR) & Andy Ram (ISR)
2005	Joachim Johansson (SWE)	Xavier Malisse (BEL) & Olivier Rochus (BEL)

NUMBER CRUNCHING

TOP 20 ALL-TIME OPEN ERA SINGLES TITLE LEADERS

* Includes ATP World Tour, Grand Prix, WCT, Grand Slam, Grand Slam Cup

1	Jimmy Connors (USA)	109
2	Ivan Lendl (USA)	94
3	John McEnroe (USA)	77
4	Pete Sampras (USA)	64
5	Bjorn Borg (SWE)	63
6	Guillermo Vilas (ARG)	62
7	Roger Federer (SUI)	61
8	Andre Agassi (USA)	60
9	Ilie Nastase (ROM)	57
10	Boris Becker (GER)	49
11	Rod Laver (AUS)	47
12	Thomas Muster (AUT)	44
13	Stefan Edberg (SWE)	41
14	Stan Smith (USA)	39
15	Rafael Nadal (ESP)	36
16	Michael Chang (USA)	34
=17	Arthur Ashe (USA)	33
	Mats Wilander (SWE)	33
=19	John Newcombe (AUS)	32
	Manuel Orantes (ESP)	32
	Ken Rosewall (AUS)	32

JIMMY CONNORS

JANUARY 11-16 | AUCKLAND, NEW ZEALAND

HEINEKEN OPEN

TOURNAMENT WEBSITE:
www.heinekenopen.co.nz

Draw: Singles-28 Doubles-16
Prize money: $355,500
Surface: Hard
Venue: ASB Tennis Centre
Tournament director: Richard Palmer
First held: 1956

The Heineken Open is a hugely popular stop on the ATP World Tour amid the breathtaking scenery of New Zealand. The country's army of tennis fans won't have realised at the time, but as they watched Argentina's Juan Martin Del Potro beat American Sam Querrey in last year's final on the hard courts of the ASB Tennis Centre, they were watching a Grand Slam champion in the making. The Auckland trophy was the fifth piece of ATP World Tour silverware Del Potro had collected during his young career and it provided the perfect springboard for what was to become truly a year to remember for the powerful South American. Del Potro added his name to a high-quality list of champions dating back to 1956 that includes the likes of Bjorn Borg, Gustavo Kuerten and Marcelo Rios.

JUAN MARTIN DEL POTRO

PAST CHAMPIONS

YEAR	SINGLES	DOUBLES
2009	Juan Martin Del Potro (ARG)	Martin Damm (CZE) & Robert Lindstedt (SWE)
2008	Philipp Kohlschreiber (GER)	Luis Horna (PER) & Juan Monaco (ARG)
2007	David Ferrer (ESP)	Jeff Coetzee (GER) & Rogier Wassen (NED)
2006	Jarkko Nieminen (FIN)	Andrei Pavel (ROM) & Rogier Wassen (NED)
2005	Fernando Gonzalez (CHI)	Yves Allegro (SUI) & Michael Kohlmann (GER)

JANUARY 11-16 | SYDNEY, AUSTRALIA

MEDIBANK INTERNATIONAL

TOURNAMENT WEBSITE:
www.medibankinternational.com.au

Draw: Singles-28 Doubles-16
Prize money: $372,500
Surface: Hard
Venue: Sydney Olympic Park Tennis Centre
Tournament director: Craig Watson
First held: 1885

The Medibank International is a combined ATP World Tour 250 tournament and Sony Ericsson WTA Tour Premier event dating back to 1885 and featuring the best men and women in the world the week before the first major of the year, the Australian Open, kicks off in Melbourne. Appropriately enough, home favourite Lleyton Hewitt has enjoyed the most success at the event recently, winning the title four times in six years between 2000 and 2005. In 2009 it was the turn of Argentine David Nalbandian to taste glory at the Sydney Olympic Park Tennis Centre when he began his season in style by beating Finland's Jarkko Nieminen in the final to claim his first silverware on Australian soil and the 10th ATP World Tour title of his career.

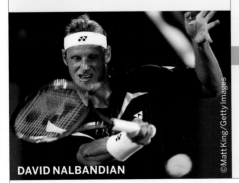
DAVID NALBANDIAN

PAST CHAMPIONS

YEAR	SINGLES	DOUBLES
2009	David Nalbandian (ARG)	Bob Bryan (USA) & Mike Bryan (USA)
2008	Dmitry Tursunov (RUS)	Richard Gasquet (FRA) & Jo-Wilfried Tsonga (FRA)
2007	James Blake (USA)	Paul Hanley (AUS) & Kevin Ullyett (RSA)
2006	James Blake (USA)	Fabrice Santoro (FRA) & Nenad Zimonjic (SRB)
2005	Lleyton Hewitt (AUS)	Mahesh Bhupathi (IND) & Todd Woodbridge (AUS)

JANUARY 18-31 | MELBOURNE, AUSTRALIA

AUSTRALIAN OPEN

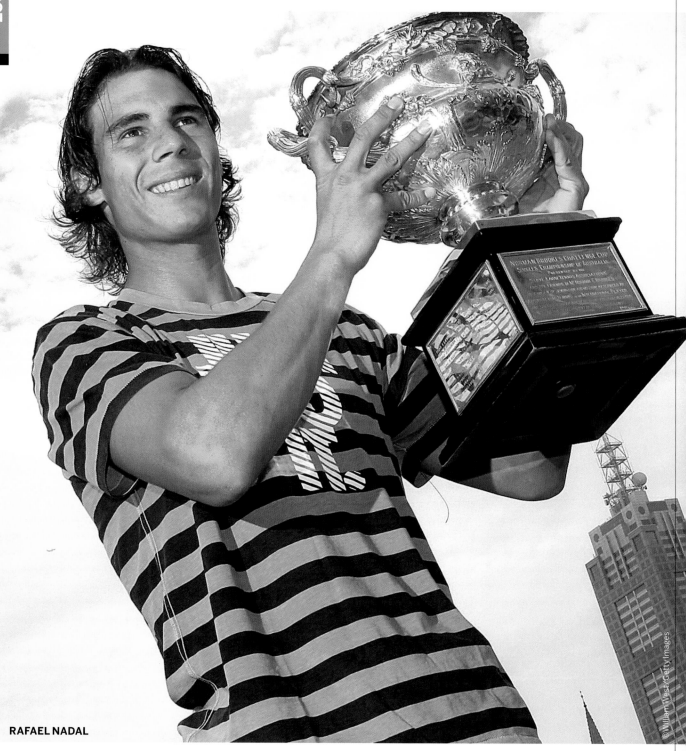

RAFAEL NADAL

Draw: Singles-128 Doubles-64
Prize money: AUS $24,094,000
Surface: Hard
Venue: Melbourne Park
Tournament director: Craig Tiley
First held: 1905

australian open
The Grand Slam of Asia/Pacific

GRAND SLAM®
(2000 POINTS)

TOURNAMENT WEBSITE:
www.australianopen.com

> **" With its early slot in the calendar, there are often surprise results with Baghdatis, Schuettler and Clement all recent finalists "**

The focus shifts to Australia early in the season as the first Grand Slam of the year gets under way midway through January at Melbourne Park. With the calendar just two weeks old, the best men and women on the planet line up for the first of four majors during the year, played under bright blue skies and in blistering temperatures where only the fittest survive.

Given its early slot in the season, the Australian Open has in the past thrown up some shock results with Jo-Wilfried Tsonga (2008), Marcos Baghdatis (2006), Rainer Schuettler (2003) and Arnaud Clement (2001) all surprise finalists.

The event was treated to a blockbuster of a final in 2009 when Rafael Nadal and Roger Federer went toe-to-toe. World No.1 and top seed Nadal had emerged from a marathon five-set semi-final with fellow Spaniard Fernando Verdasco (the longest match in the tournament's history at five hours and 14 minutes) and recorded back-to-back five-set victories by outlasting Federer 75 36 76(3) 36 62 in a final that stretched well over four hours. The victory earned him his first Grand Slam on a hard court, his sixth in total and made him the first Spanish singles champion at the Australian Open.

PAST **CHAMPIONS**

YEAR	SINGLES	DOUBLES
2009	Rafael Nadal (ESP)	Bob Bryan (USA) & Mike Bryan (USA)
2008	Novak Djokovic (SRB)	Jonathan Erlich (ISR) Andy Ram (ISR)
2007	Roger Federer (SUI)	Bob Bryan (USA) & Mike Bryan (USA)
2006	Roger Federer (SUI)	Bob Bryan (USA) & Mike Bryan (USA)
2005	Marat Safin (RUS)	Wayne Black (ZIM) & Kevin Ullyett (ZIM)
2004	Roger Federer (SUI)	Michael Llodra (FRA) & Fabrice Santoro (FRA)
2003	Andre Agassi (USA)	Michael Llodra (FRA) & Fabrice Santoro (FRA)
2002	Thomas Johansson (SWE)	Mark Knowles (BAH) & Daniel Nestor (CAN)
2001	Andre Agassi (USA)	Jonas Bjorkman (SWE) & Todd Woodbridge (AUS)
2000	Andre Agassi (USA)	Ellis Ferreira (RSA) & Rick Leach (USA)

BRYAN BROTHERS

FEBRUARY 1-7 | SANTIAGO, CHILE

MOVISTAR OPEN

TOURNAMENT WEBSITE:
www.movistaropen.cl

Draw: Singles-32, Doubles-16
Prize money: $398,250
Surface: Clay
Venue: Hacienda Chicureo-Piedra Roja-Colina
Tournament director: Alvaro Fillol
First held: 1993

Held in Vina Del Mar from 2001-2009, the Movistar Open will return to its very first host city, Santiago, in 2010 and fiery Chilean Fernando Gonzalez will be back aiming for a hat-trick of titles having triumphed at the clay court event in 2008 and 2009. The tournament is the first clay court get-together of the ATP World Tour calendar and gets the so-called 'Golden Swing' under way, four weeks of South American clay court tournaments that see some of the world's best players visit Chile, Brazil, Argentina and Mexico. Some real clay court giants have won this event over the years including two former French Open champions – Brazilian Gustavo Kuerten in 2000 and Argentine Gaston Gaudio five years later.

FERNANDO GONZALEZ
©AFP/Getty Images

PAST CHAMPIONS

YEAR	SINGLES	DOUBLES
2009	Fernando Gonzalez (CHI)	Pablo Cuevas (URU) & Brian Dabul (ARG)
2008	Fernando Gonzalez (CHI)	Jose Acasuso (ARG) & Sebastian Prieto (ARG)
2007	Luis Horna (PER)	Paul Capdeville (CHI) & Oscar Hernandez (ESP)
2006	Jose Acasuso (ARG)	Jose Acasuso (ARG) & Sebastian Prieto (ARG)
2005	Gaston Gaudio (ARG)	David Ferrer (ESP) & Santiago Ventura (ESP)

FEBRUARY 1-7 | ZAGREB, CROATIA

PBZ ZAGREB INDOORS

PBZ ZAGREB INDOORS

TOURNAMENT WEBSITE:
www.zagrebindoors.com

Draw: Singles-32, Doubles-16
Prize money: €398,250
Surface: Indoor Hard
Venue: Dom Sportova
Tournament director: Branimir Horvat
First held: 2006

One of the youngest ATP World Tour events on the calendar, the PBZ Zagreb Indoors will celebrate its fifth edition at the Dom Sportova stadium in the first week of February and signals the start of a three-week run of European indoor hard court tournaments that will see the stars visit Croatia, the Netherlands and France. The local fans were treated to a home-grown champion when Ivan Ljubicic lifted the trophy at the inaugural staging of the event back in 2006 and another Croatian, Marin Cilic, made sure the silverware stayed on home soil once again when he beat countryman Mario Ancic in the 2009 final. Cilic, who picked up two ATP World tour titles in 2009, will be back in Zagreb in 2010 hoping to continue the local success at what is the first European tournament of the ATP World Tour calendar.

MARIN CILIC
©Rene Karaman

PAST CHAMPIONS

YEAR	SINGLES	DOUBLES
2009	Marin Cilic (CRO)	Martin Damm (CZE) & Robert Lindstedt (SWE)
2008	Sergiy Stakhovsky (UKR)	Paul Hanley (AUS) & Jordan Kerr (AUS)
2007	Marcos Baghdatis (CYP)	Michael Kohlmann (GER) & Alexander Waske (GER)
2006	Ivan Ljubicic (CRO)	Jaroslav Levinsky (CZE) & Michal Mertinak (SVK)

TICKET INFO: Visit www.satennis.co.za

FEBRUARY 1-7 | JOHANNESBURG, SOUTH AFRICA

SA TENNIS OPEN

TOURNAMENT WEBSITE:
www.satennis.co.za

Draw: Singles-32, Doubles-16
Prize money: $442,500
Surface: Hard
Venue: Montecasino, Johannesburg
Tournament director: Ian Smith
First held: 2009

ATP World Tour tennis returned to Johannesburg for the first time in 13 years when the inaugural SA Tennis Open kicked off in February 2009. The brand new event was blessed with some entertaining matches in its first year and a charismatic champion in the shape of explosive Frenchman Jo-Wilfried Tsonga who raced to the title without dropping a single set. The tournament is held in the impressive grounds of the Montecasino complex, in the northern suburbs of the city, which boasts two fantastic, purpose-built show courts with enough room for 6,000 tennis fans. The retail and entertainment complex also features a 15-screen cinema complex, a skate park and the star attraction, the Montecasino Bird Gardens.

JO-WILFRIED TSONGA

(L-R) JAMES CERRETANI & DICK NORMAN

PAST CHAMPIONS

YEAR	SINGLES	DOUBLES
2009	Jo-Wilfried Tsonga (FRA)	James Cerretani (USA) & Dick Norman (BEL)

TICKET INFO: Call +55-11-5643-5511 or visit www2.uol.com.br/tenisbrasil/brasilopen

FEBRUARY 8-14 | COSTA DO SAUIPE, BRAZIL

BRASIL OPEN

TOURNAMENT WEBSITE:
www2.uol.com.br/tenisbrasil/brasilopen

Draw: Singles-32 Doubles-16
Prize money: $442,500
Surface: Clay
Venue: Costa do Sauipe-Salvador
Tournament director: Luis Felipe Tavares
First held: 2001

Held in the coastal city of Salvador, in the north-east of the country, the Brasil Open is another South American clay court tournament with a long list of high-quality former champions. The likes of Grand Slam winners Gustavo Kuerten and Rafael Nadal have both won the ATP World Tour 250 event since it was first held back in 2001. Another Spaniard, Tommy Robredo, reigned in 2009 when he won the eighth singles title of his career and left with the doubles trophy too after success alongside countryman Marcel Granollers. The tournament is held yards away from some of Brazil's most stunning beaches and is known for its environmental efforts. Since it began, organisers have planted 500 trees to neutralise carbon emissions and each year provide recyclable materials to local children for use in craft work.

PAST CHAMPIONS

YEAR	SINGLES	DOUBLES
2009	Tommy Robredo (ESP)	Marcel Granollers (ESP) & Tommy Robredo (ESP)
2008	Nicolas Almagro (ESP)	Marcelo Melo (BRA) & Andre Sa (BRA)
2007	Guillermo Canas (ARG)	Lukas Dlouhy (CZE) & Pavel Vizner (CZE)
2006	Nicolas Massu (CHI)	Lukas Dlouhy (CZE) & Pavel Vizner (CZE)
2005	Rafael Nadal (ESP)	Frantisek Cermak (CZE) & Leos Friedl (ARG)

FEBRUARY 8-14 | ROTTERDAM, THE NETHERLANDS

ABN AMRO WORLD TENNIS TOURNAMENT

TOURNAMENT WEBSITE:
www.abnamrowtt.nl

Draw: Singles-32 Doubles-16
Prize money: €1,150,000
Surface: Indoor Hard
Venue: Ahoy Stadium
Tournament director: Richard Krajicek
First held: 1974

It was appropriate that Dutch great Tom Okker was the first winner of the ABN AMRO World Tennis Tournament back in 1974 but Rotterdam's tennis fans had to wait a long time until they cheered the next home-grown champion onto the winner's podium at the Ahoy Stadium. Twenty-one years later Richard Krajicek ended the wait when he lifted the trophy in 1995, and the former Wimbledon champion is now, rather appropriately, the tournament director at the ATP World Tour 500 event, which has been one of the biggest indoor get-togethers on the calendar since it first began.

Legends such as Arthur Ashe, Jimmy Connors, Björn Borg, Boris Becker, Stefan Edberg and Roger Federer have all ruled the roost in Rotterdam and it was Andy Murray who became the first British champion in 2009 when he got the better of Rafael Nadal in a three-set final.

The tournament has always been a popular venue for European tennis fans – the first edition attracted 46,000 spectators and in the last two years more than 100,000 have poured through the gates each week.

(L-R) ANDY MURRAY & RAFAEL NADAL

ROTTERDAM

(L-R) NENAD ZIMONJIC & DANIEL NESTOR

PAST **CHAMPIONS**

YEAR	SINGLES	DOUBLES
2009	Andy Murray (GBR)	Daniel Nestor (CAN) & Nenad Zimonjic (SRB)
2008	Michael Llodra (FRA)	Tomas Berdych (CZE) & Dmitry Tursunov (RUS)
2007	Mikhail Youzhny (RUS)	Martin Damm (CZE) & Leander Paes (IND)
2006	Radek Stepanek (CZE)	Paul Hanley (AUS) & Kevin Ullyett (ZIM)
2005	Roger Federer (SUI)	Jonathan Erlich (ISR) & Andy Ram (ISR)
2004	Lleyton Hewitt (AUS)	Paul Hanley (AUS) & Radek Stepanek (CZE)
2003	Max Mirnyi (BLR)	Wayne Arthurs (AUS) & Paul Hanley (AUS)
2002	Nicolas Escude (FRA)	Roger Federer (SUI) & Max Mirnyi (BLR)
2001	Nicolas Escude (FRA)	Jonas Bjorkman (SWE) & Roger Federer (SUI)
2000	Cedric Pioline (FRA)	David Adams (RSA) & John-Laffnie de Jager (RSA)

FEBRUARY 8-14 | SAN JOSE, CALIFORNIA, USA

SAP OPEN

TOURNAMENT WEBSITE:
www.sapopentennis.com

Draw: Singles-32 Doubles-16
Prize money: $531,000
Surface: Hard
Venue: HP Pavilion at San Jose
Tournament director: Bill A. Rapp
First held: 1889

Dating way back to 1889, the SAP Open is the second oldest tournament in the United States and has a rich history of big name former champions. The likes of Grand Slam winners Bjorn Borg, John McEnroe, Ivan Lendl, Stefan Edberg and Michael Chang have all won this outdoor hard court event and in recent years more greats such as Pete Sampras, Andre Agassi, Lleyton Hewitt, Andy Murray and Andy Roddick have joined the list. In 2009 it was the turn of Czech thirtysomething Radek Stepanek to show the younger guys a thing or two by winning his second singles trophy inside a month when he beat home favourite Mardy Fish in the final. Stepanek also left with the doubles trophy as well after winning alongside German Tommy Haas.

PAST **CHAMPIONS**

YEAR	SINGLES	DOUBLES
2009	Radek Stepanek (CZE)	Tommy Haas (GER) & Radek Stepanek (CZE)
2008	Andy Roddick (USA)	Scott Lipsky (USA) & David Martin (USA)
2007	Andy Murray (GBR)	Eric Butorac (USA) & Jamie Murray (GBR)
2006	Andy Murray (GBR)	Jonas Bjorkman (SWE) & John McEnroe (USA)
2005	Andy Roddick (USA)	Wayne Arthurs (AUS) & Paul Hanley (AUS)

FEBRUARY 15-21 | MARSEILLE, FRANCE

OPEN 13

TOURNAMENT WEBSITE:
www.open13.fr

Draw: Singles-28, Doubles-16
Prize money: €512,750
Surface: Indoor Hard
Venue: Palais des Sports
Tournament director:
Jean-François Caujolle
First held: 1993

JO-WILFRIED TSONGA

The Open 13 is the first of five ATP World Tour events to be held in France throughout the year and brings to a close a brief, three-week run of springtime indoor European tournaments. French fans visiting the Palais des Sports over the years have enjoyed watching plenty of home-grown success and they roared another of their own on to victory in 2009 when Jo-Wilfried Tsonga lifted the cup after beating countryman Michael Llodra in the final. The man from Le Mans joined the likes of Guy Forget, Fabrice Santoro, Arnaud Clement and Gilles Simon in the list of Frenchman to have won the ATP World Tour 250 held on the Mediterranean coast. Llodra didn't leave empty-handed, however, when he teamed up with another Frenchman, Arnaud Clement, to take the doubles title.

PAST **CHAMPIONS**

YEAR	SINGLES	DOUBLES
2009	Jo-Wilfried Tsonga (FRA)	Arnaud Clement (FRA) & Michael Llodra (FRA)
2008	Andy Murray (GBR)	Martin Damm (CZE) & Pavel Vizner (CZE)
2007	Gilles Simon (FRA)	Arnaud Clement (FRA) & Michael Llodra (FRA)
2006	Arnaud Clement (FRA)	Martin Damm (CZE) & Radek Stepanek (CZE)
2005	Joachim Johansson (SWE)	Martin Damm (CZE) & Radek Stepanek (CZE)

FEBRUARY 15-21 | MEMPHIS, TENNESSEE, USA

REGIONS MORGAN KEEGAN CHAMPIONSHIPS

Sony Ericsson
WTA TOUR

TOURNAMENT WEBSITE:
www.memphistennis.com

ATP WORLD TOUR **500**

Draw: Singles-32 Doubles-16
Prize money: $1,100,000
Surface: Indoor hard
Venue: The Racquet Club of Memphis
Tournament director: Peter Lebedevs
First held: 1976

This ATP World Tour 500 event, the second of 11 on the ATP World Tour calendar, is held in the luxurious surroundings of The Racquet Club of Memphis, the only private club to host a professional men's and women's combined indoor event. The tournament began in 1976 and soon became the U.S. Indoor National Championships, which was first won by the great Bjorn Borg in 1977. The Swede was one of the first superstars to win the tournament and many followed in the years to come, with legends such as Jimmy Connors, John McEnroe, Stefan Edberg, Ivan Lendl, Andre Agassi, Jim Courier, Pete Sampras and Andy Roddick adding their names to the honour roll.

In 2001 the club bought the franchise rights to a Sony Ericsson WTA Tour event and for the last nine years fans have been able to enjoy watching the best women in the world as well as the men. Roddick first won the event back in 2002 but captured his second trophy in Tennessee in 2009 when he beat Czech Radek Stepanek in the American's fourth appearance in a Memphis singles final.

ANDY RODDICK

©Torsten Blackwood/AFP/Getty Images

MARK KNOWLES

©Elsa/Getty Images

PAST **CHAMPIONS**

YEAR	SINGLES	DOUBLES
2009	Andy Roddick (USA)	Mardy Fish (USA) & Mark Knowles (BAH)
2008	Steve Darcis (BEL)	Mahesh Bhupathi (IND) & Mark Knowles (BAH)
2007	Tommy Haas (GER)	Eric Butorac (USA) & Jamie Murray (GBR)
2006	Tommy Haas (GER)	Chris Haggard (RSA) & Ivo Karlovic (CRO)
2005	Kenneth Carlsen (DEN)	Simon Aspelin (SWE) & Todd Perry (AUS)
2004	Joachim Johansson (SWE)	Bob Bryan (USA) & Mike Bryan (USA)
2003	Taylor Dent (USA)	Mark Knowles (BAH) & Daniel Nestor (CAN)
2002	Andy Roddick (USA)	Brian MacPhie (USA) & Nenad Zimonjic (SRB)
2001	Mark Philippoussis (AUS)	Bob Bryan (USA) & Mike Bryan (USA)
2000	Magnus Larsson (SWE)	Justin Gimelstob (USA) & Sebastien Lareau (CAN)

FEBRUARY 15-21 | BUENOS AIRES, ARGENTINA
COPA TELMEX

COPA **TELMEX**

250 ATP WORLD TOUR

TOURNAMENT WEBSITE:
www.copatelmex.com

Draw: Singles-32 Doubles-16
Prize money: $475,300
Surface: Clay
Venue: Buenos Aires Lawn Tennis Club
Tournament director: Martin Jaite
First held: 2001

The third of four springtime South American clay court tournaments that form the so-called 'Golden Swing', the Copa Telmex has an illustrious list of past champions. Spain's former world No.1 Carlos Moya will have fond memories of his visits to the Buenos Aires Lawn Tennis Club, also known as the "Cathedral of Argentine tennis", having lifted the cup four times in nine years. Another two former Grand Slam champions – Brazil's Gustavo Kuerten and Argentine Gaston Gaudio – have also won in Buenos Aires, and it was Spain's Tommy Robredo who ruled in 2009 when he beat 2007 champion Juan Monaco in the final. It was Robredo's second trophy in as many weeks after arriving in Argentina hot on the heels of a title at the Brasil Open.

PAST CHAMPIONS

YEAR	SINGLES	DOUBLES
2009	Tommy Robredo (ESP)	Marcel Granollers (ESP) & Alberto Martin (ESP)
2008	David Nalbandian (ARG)	Agustin Calleri (ARG) & Luis Horna (PER)
2007	Juan Monaco (ARG)	Martin Garcia (ARG) & Sebastian Prieto (ARG)
2006	Carlos Moya (ESP)	Frantisek Cermak (CZE) & Leos Friedl (CZE)
2005	Gaston Gaudio (ARG)	Frantisek Cermak (CZE) & Leos Friedl (CZE)

ROGER FEDERER

NUMBER CRUNCHING

TOTAL CAREER PRIZE MONEY LEADERS

* As of Dec 7 2009

1	Roger Federer	$53,362,068
2	Pete Sampras	$43,280,489
3	Andre Agassi	$31,152,975
4	Rafael Nadal	$27,224,163
5	Boris Becker	$25,080,956
6	Yevgeny Kafelnikov	$23,883,797
7	Ivan Lendl	$21,262,417
8	Stefan Edberg	$20,630,941
9	Goran Ivanisevic	$19,876,579
10	Michael Chang	$19,145,632
11	Lleyton Hewitt	$18,312,036
12	Andy Roddick	$17,109,084
13	Novak Djokovic	$15,984,098
14	Gustavo Kuerten	$14,807,000
15	Jonas Bjorkman	$14,600,323
16	Marat Safin	$14,373,291
17	Jim Courier	$14,034,132
18	Carlos Moya	$13,382,822
19	Nikolay Davydenko	$13,239,499
20	Michael Stich	$12,595,128

FEBRUARY 22-27 | ACAPULCO, MEXICO

Sony Ericsson WTA TOUR

abierto mexicano *telcel* presentado por HSBC ◆

ABIERTO MEXICANO TELCEL
PRESENTED BY HSBC

ATP WORLD TOUR 500

TOURNAMENT WEBSITE:
www.abiertomexicanodetenis.com

Draw: Singles-32 Doubles-16
Prize money: $955,000
Surface: Clay
Venue: The Fairmont Acapulco Princess
Tournament director: Raul Zurutuza
First held: 1993

The Abierto Mexicano Telcel boasts one of the most breathtaking venues of any of the 11 ATP World Tour 500 events, held yards from Revolcadero Beach on Mexico's Pacific Coast, on the clay courts of the Fairmont Acapulco Princess hotel and resort. The combined ATP World Tour and Sony Ericsson WTA Tour event, which moved to Acapulco in 2001, brings to a climax the so-called "Golden Swing" of four Latin American clay court events that take place throughout February.

The Abierto Mexicano Telcel won the ATP World Tour award for best tournament of the year in its category in 2007 and has attracted a world-class field since it first began in 1993. Three-time French Open champion Gustavo Kuerten, former world No.1 Carlos Moya and six-time Grand Slam champion Rafael Nadal all lifted the trophy between the years of 2001 and 2005, but it is another Spaniard, Nicolas Almagro, who has made the tournament his own recently, winning back-to-back titles in 2008 and 2009. The man from Murcia beat Frenchman Gael Monfils in the 2009 final to became the first player to capture back-to-back titles since Austrian Thomas Muster won four in a row from 1993-96 in Mexico City.

NICOLAS ALMAGRO

NICOLAS ALMAGRO

(L-R) FRANTISEK CERMAK & MICHAL MERTINAK

PAST **CHAMPIONS**

YEAR	SINGLES	DOUBLES
2009	Nicolas Almagro (ESP)	Frantisek Cermak (CZE) & Michal Mertinak (SVK)
2008	Nicolas Almagro (ESP)	Oliver Marach (AUT) & Michal Mertinak (SVK)
2007	Juan Ignacio Chela (ARG)	Potito Starace (ITA) & Martin Vassallo Arguello (ARG)
2006	Luis Horna (PER)	Frantisek Cermak (CZE) & Leos Friedl (CZE)
2005	Rafael Nadal (ESP)	David Ferrer (ESP) & Santiago Ventura (ESP)
2004	Carlos Moya (ESP)	Bob Bryan (USA) & Mike Bryan (USA)
2003	Agustin Calleri (ARG)	Mark Knowles (BAH) & Daniel Nestor (CAN)
2002	Carlos Moya (ESP)	Bob Bryan (USA) & Mike Bryan (USA)
2001	Gustavo Kuerten (ESP)	Donald Johnson (USA) & Gustavo Kuerten (BRA)
2000	Juan Ignacio Chela (ARG)	Byron Black (ZIM) & Donald Johnson (USA)

SOUTH AFRICAN AIRWAYS
A STAR ALLIANCE MEMBER

Our milestones. Your memories.

London - Cape Town: Enormous comfort

One daily nonstop overnight flight from London Heathrow with South African Airways to Cape Town. Relax in an award winning flat bed in Premium Class or enjoy ample legroom in Economy Class while sampling some of the finest wines around. Once in South Africa, we'll connect you to more domestic and regional destinations than any other scheduled carrier in Africa. Call 020 8576 5555 or visit f l y s a a . c o m

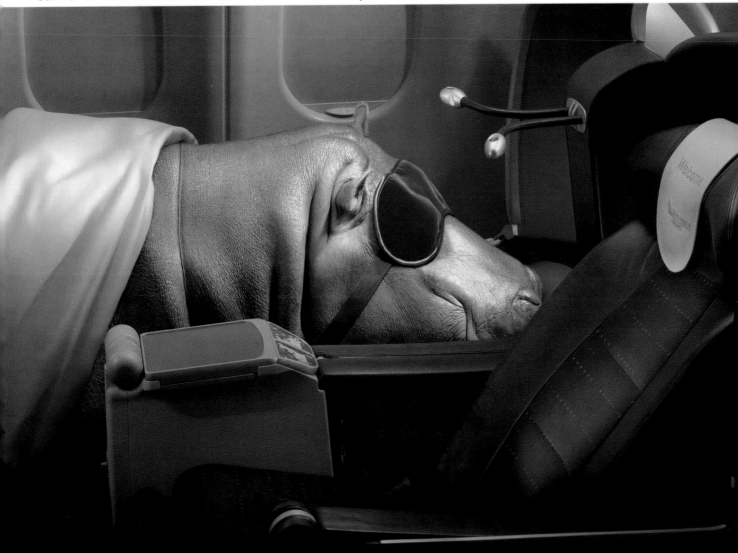

South African Airways, the experts choice

ATP WORLD TOUR 500

BARCLAYS DUBAI TENNIS CHAMPIONSHIPS

TOURNAMENT WEBSITE:
www.barclaysdubaitennischampionships.com

Draw: Singles-32 Doubles-16
Prize money: $1,619,500
Surface: Hard
Venue: Dubai Stadium
Tournament director:
Salah Hussain Bin Tahlak
First held: 1993

The Barclays Dubai Tennis Championships has been welcoming the world's very best players since it was first staged in 1993 so it is perhaps appropriate that Swiss Roger Federer holds the record for the most titles won having claimed the Dubai trophy four times in five years between 2003 and 2007. The fourth ATP World Tour 500 event of the year takes place every February at the Aviation Club Tennis Centre inside the impressive 5,000-seat Dubai Tennis Stadium, which has been home to the tournament for the last 17 years.

Serbian Novak Djokovic was the most recent star to add his name to the honour roll when he won his first title in the United Arab Emirates in 2009 with a straight sets win over Spain's David Ferrer. "Winning the tournament, any tournament, is a huge success, and especially here in Dubai, which has a history of being one of the strongest events in the tour," Djokovic said.

NOVAK DJOKOVIC

DUBAI

©Julian Finney/Getty Images

©Karim Sahib/AFP/Getty Images

©Barclays Dubai Tennis Championships

PAST **CHAMPIONS**

YEAR	SINGLES	DOUBLES
2009	Novak Djokovic (SRB)	Rik De Voest (RSA) & Dmitry Tursunov (RUS)
2008	Andy Roddick (USA)	Mahesh Bhupathi (IND) & Mark Knowles (BAH)
2007	Roger Federer (SUI)	Fabrice Santoro (FRA) & Nenad Zimonjic (SRB)
2006	Rafael Nadal (ESP)	Paul Hanley (AUS) & Kevin Ullyett (ZIM)
2005	Roger Federer (SUI)	Martin Damm (CZE) & Radek Stepanek (CZE)
2004	Roger Federer (SUI)	Mahesh Bhupathi (IND) & Fabrice Santoro (FRA)
2003	Roger Federer (SUI)	Leander Paes (IND) & David Rikl (CZE)
2002	Fabrice Santoro (FRA)	Mark Knowles (BAH) & Daniel Nestor (CAN)
2001	Juan Carlos Ferrero (ESP)	Joshua Eagle (AUS) & Sandon Stolle (AUS)
2000	Nicolas Kiefer (GER)	Jiri Novak (CZE) & David Rikl (CZE)

FEBRUARY 22-28 | DELRAY BEACH, FLORIDA, USA

DELRAY BEACH
INTERNATIONAL TENNIS CHAMPIONSHIPS

DELRAY BEACH
INTERNATIONAL TENNIS CHAMPIONSHIPS
YELLOWTENNISBALL.COM

TOURNAMENT WEBSITE:
www.YellowTennisBall.com

Draw: Singles-32 Doubles-16
Prize money: $442,500
Surface: Hard
Venue: Delray Beach Stadium & Tennis Center
Tournament director: Mark S. Baron
First held: 1993

Americans enjoyed a clean sweep of titles at the 2009 Delray Beach International Tennis Championships, an outdoor hard court ATP World Tour 250 that takes its place in the calendar directly before back-to-back ATP World Tour Masters 1000s in Indian Wells, California, and Miami, Florida. Mardy Fish became the first top seed to hoist the singles trophy aloft in the event's 17-year history and the Bryan brothers walked away with the doubles crown. This popular stop for fans and players began as a red clay court tournament before moving to the hard courts of the Delray Beach Stadium & Tennis Center, in Palm Beach County, six years later. Among its former champions are Todd Martin, former world No.1 Lleyton Hewitt and Tommy Haas.

MARDY FISH

PAST **CHAMPIONS**

YEAR	SINGLES	DOUBLES
2009	Mardy Fish (USA)	Bob Bryan (USA) & Mike Bryan (USA)
2008	Kei Nishikori (JAP)	Max Mirnyi (BLR) & Jamie Murray (GBR)
2007	Xavier Malisse (BEL)	Hugo Armando (USA) & Xavier Malisse (BEL)
2006	Tommy Haas (GER)	Mark Knowles (BAH) & Daniel Nestor (CAN)
2005	Xavier Malisse (BEL)	Simon Aspelin (SWE) & Todd Perry (AUS)

NUMBER CRUNCHING

ATP WORLD TOUR MASTERS 1000 CAREER TITLE LEADERS

There have been 55 different winners of ATP World Tour Masters 1000s since 1990; of those winners, 32 have won more than one title.

Andre Agassi (USA)	17
Roger Federer (SUI)	16
Rafael Nadal (ESP)	15
Pete Sampras (USA)	11
Thomas Muster (AUT)	8
Michael Chang (USA)	7
Boris Becker (GER)	5
Jim Courier (USA)	5
Novak Djokovic (SRB)	5
Gustavo Kuerten (BRA)	5
Marcelo Rios (CHI)	5
Marat Safin (RUS)	5
Stefan Edberg (SWE)	4
Juan Carlos Ferrero (ESP)	4
Andrei Medvedev (UKR)	4
Andy Murray (GBR)	4
Andy Roddick (USA)	4
Nikolay Davydenko (RUS)	3
Thomas Enqvist (SWE)	3
Carlos Moya (ESP)	3

ANDRE AGASSI

MARCH 11-21 | INDIAN WELLS, CALIFORNIA, USA

BNP PARIBAS OPEN

ATP WORLD TOUR
MASTERS 1000

RAFAEL NADAL

©Robyn Beck/Getty Images

Draw: Singles-96 Doubles-32
Prize money: $3,645,000
Surface: Hard
Venue: Indian Wells Tennis Garden
Tournament director: Charlie Pasarell
First held: 1976

Sony Ericsson
WTA TOUR

TOURNAMENT WEBSITE:
www.bnpparibasopen.org

> Indian Wells boasts a 16,100-capacity centre court, the second largest purpose-built tennis stadium in the world

The BNP Paribas Open, held at the Indian Wells Tennis Garden, boasts one of the most stunning backdrops of any tennis venue – the Santa Rosa Mountains in Southern California. It's no surprise then that this event – the first ATP World Tour Masters 1000 of the year – is a popular stop for fans, highlighted by the attendance figure for 2009. Last year a record 332,498 people swarmed through the turnstiles during the 12-day hard court event. The Tennis Garden boasts a spectacular 16,100-capacity centre court, the second largest purpose-built tennis stadium in the world behind the Arthur Ashe Stadium at Flushing Meadows. The tournament, which in 2007 became the first outside a Grand Slam to attract more than 300,000 fans, will celebrate its 35th birthday in 2010 and will once again play host to the best tennis players on the planet. Spain's Rafael Nadal will be back aiming to defend the crown he won 12 months earlier when he beat Andy Murray in the final. The Spaniard is one of a long, illustrious list of former champions – Roger Federer, Andre Agassi, Pete Sampras, Jim Courier, Stefan Edberg, Boris Becker and Jimmy Connors have all won here.

PAST **CHAMPIONS**

YEAR	SINGLES	DOUBLES
2009	**Rafael Nadal** (ESP)	**Mardy Fish** (USA) & **Andy Roddick** (USA)
2008	**Novak Djokovic** (SRB)	**Jonathan Erlich** (ISR) & **Andy Ram** (ISR)
2007	**Rafael Nadal** (ESP)	**Martin Damm** (CZE) & **Lenader Paes** (IND)
2006	**Roger Federer** (SUI)	**Mark Knowles** (BAH) & **Daniel Nestor** (CAN)
2005	**Roger Federer** (SUI)	**Mark Knowles** (BAH) & **Daniel Nestor** (CAN)
2004	**Roger Federer** (SUI)	**Arnaud Clement** (FRA) & **Sebastien Grosjean** (FRA)
2003	**Lleyton Hewitt** (AUS)	**Wayne Ferreira** (RSA) & **Yevgeny Kafelnikov** (RUS)
2002	**Lleyton Hewitt** (AUS)	**Mark Knowles** (BAH) & **Daniel Nestor** (CAN)
2001	**Andre Agassi** (USA)	**Wayne Ferreira** (RSA) & **Yevgeny Kafelnikov** (RUS)
2000	**Alex Corretja** (ESP)	**Alex O'Brien** (USA) & **Jared Palmer** (USA)

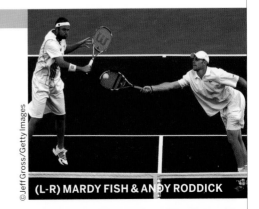

(L-R) MARDY FISH & ANDY RODDICK

MARCH 24-APRIL 4 | MIAMI, FLORIDA, USA

SONY ERICSSON OPEN

" Since the event began in 1985, one legend after another has added their name to the champions' roll of honour "

The Sony Ericsson Open is one of the calendar's biggest and most important events and boasts a rich heritage. Like the BNP Paribas Open in Indian Wells that comes before it, the tournament features the best men and women in the world as a combined ATP World Tour and Sony Ericsson WTA Tour event, dating back to 1985 when Tim Mayotte and Martina Navratilova were crowned the first ever champions.

Since then, one legend after another has added their name to the roll of honour. American Andre Agassi holds the most men's titles, having lifted the famous trophy an incredible six times during his career. His last victory in 2003 made him the tournament's oldest champion at 32 years and 11 months and he also holds the event's best win-loss record with a 59-10 statistic. Andy Murray became the first-ever British champion in 2009 when he capped a fine fortnight by beating 2007 champion Novak Djokovic in the final 62 75.

The tournament is also distinctive in terms of embracing ground-breaking technology since it was the first US event in 2006 to introduce an official review system, allowing players to challenge line-calls.

PAST **CHAMPIONS**

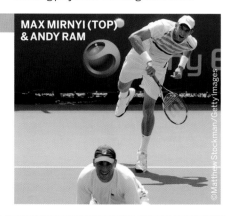

MAX MIRNYI (TOP) & ANDY RAM

YEAR	SINGLES	DOUBLES
2009	Andy Murray (GBR)	Max Mirnyi (BLR) & Andy Ram (ISR)
2008	Nikolay Davydenko (RUS)	Bob Bryan (USA) & Mike Bryan (USA)
2007	Novak Djokovic (SER)	Bob Bryan (USA) & Mike Bryan (USA)
2006	Roger Federer (SUI)	Jonas Bjorkman (SWE) & Max Mirnyi (BLR)
2005	Roger Federer (SUI)	Jonas Bjorkman (SWE) & Max Mirnyi (BLR)
2004	Andy Roddick (USA)	Wayne Black (ZIM) & Kevin Ullyett (ZIM)
2003	Andre Agassi (USA)	Roger Federer (SUI) & Max Mirnyi (BLR)
2002	Andre Agassi (USA)	Mark Knowles (BAH) & Daniel Nestor (CAN)
2001	Andre Agassi (USA)	Jiri Novak (CZE) & David Rikl (CZE)
2000	Pete Sampras (USA)	Todd Woodbridge (AUS) & Mark Woodforde (AUS)

Draw: Singles-96 Doubles-32
Prize money: $3,645,000
Surface: Hard
Venue: Tennis Center at Crandon Park
Tournament director: Adam Barrett
First held: 1985

Sony Ericsson Open

Sony Ericsson
WTA TOUR

MASTERS
1000
ATP
WORLD TOUR

TOURNAMENT WEBSITE:
www.sonyericssonopen.com

ANDY MURRAY

©Al Bello/Getty Images

APRIL 5-11 | HOUSTON, TEXAS, USA

US MEN'S CLAY COURT CHAMPIONSHIP

TOURNAMENT WEBSITE:
www.mensclaycourt.com

Draw:	Singles-28, Doubles-16
Prize money:	$442,500
Surface:	Clay
Venue:	River Oaks Country Club
Tournament director:	Van D. Barry
First held:	1910

The US Men's Clay Court Championship is the only ATP World Tour event played on the surface in the United States and has welcomed some huge names to its venue, the River Oaks Country Club, in Houston, Texas, over the years. The event first began in 1910 in Omaha with the intention of encouraging the development of more clay courts in the western half of the USA and was played in numerous cities before settling at its current venue in 2001. Australian Lleyton Hewitt ruled in 2009 when he beat American Wayne Odesnik in the final to prove he was well on the way back from the hip surgery he underwent midway through 2008. The former world No.1 joined the likes of Michael Chang, Jim Courier, Andre Agassi, Tommy Haas and Andy Roddick on the singles roll of honour.

LLEYTON HEWITT

PAST **CHAMPIONS**

YEAR	SINGLES	DOUBLES
2009	Lleyton Hewitt (AUS)	Bob Bryan (USA) & Mike Bryan (USA)
2008	Marcel Granollers (ESP)	Ernests Gulbis (LAT) & Rainer Schuettler (GER)
2007	Ivo Karlovic (CRO)	Bob Bryan (USA) & Mike Bryan (USA)
2006	Mardy Fish (USA)	Michael Kohlmann (GER) & Alexander Waske (GER)
2005	Andy Roddick (USA)	Mark Knowles (BAH) & Daniel Nestor (CAN)

APRIL 5-11 | CASABLANCA, MOROCCO

GRAND PRIX HASSAN II

TOURNAMENT WEBSITE:
www.gphassan2tennis.com

Draw:	Singles-32, Doubles-16
Prize money:	€398,250
Surface:	Clay
Venue:	Complexe Sportif al Amal
Tournament director:	Khalid Outaleb
First held:	1984

The Grand Prix Hassan II is fairly unique on the ATP World Tour calendar in that it is entirely funded by a member of royalty, Morocco's King Mohammed VI. The ATP World Tour 250 clay court tournament was first played in 1984 and will celebrate its 25th anniversary in 2010. The event – along with the SA Tennis Open in Johannesburg, one of just two ATP World Tour stops on the African continent – was won by former world No.1 Juan Carlos Ferrero in 2009 after the Spaniard beat Frenchman Florent Serra to get his hands on his first singles trophy since 2003. The result kick-started Ferrero's charge back up the South African Airways ATP rankings during 2009 which left him at No.23 at the end of the season.

JUAN CARLOS FERRERO

PAST **CHAMPIONS**

YEAR	SINGLES	DOUBLES
2009	Juan Carlos Ferrero (ESP)	Lukasz Kubot (POL) & Oliver Marach (AUT)
2008	Gilles Simon (FRA)	Albert Montanes (ESP) & Santiago Ventura (ESP)
2007	Paul-Henri Mathieu (FRA)	Jordan Kerr (AUS) & David Skoch (CZE)
2006	Daniele Bracciali (ITA)	Julian Knowle (AUT) & Jurgen Melzer (AUT)
2005	Mariano Puerta (ARG)	Frantisek Cermak (CZE) & Leos Friedl (CZE)

Individual success hinges on surrounding yourself with the right people, tools and solutions.

Combined focus helps us all succeed

The inspiration is everywhere.
Moving Ideas Forward.

ATP
WORLD TOUR
OFFICIAL
PARTNER

RICOH

ricoh-europe.com   Office Solutions   Production Printing   Managed Document Services

APRIL 11-18 | MONTE-CARLO, MONACO

MONTE-CARLO ROLEX MASTERS

ATP WORLD TOUR **MASTERS 1000**

RAFAEL NADAL

©AFP/Getty Images

Draw: Singles-56 Doubles-24
Prize money: €2,227,500
Surface: Clay
Venue: Monte-Carlo Country Club
Tournament director: Zeljko Franulovic
First held: 1897

TOURNAMENT WEBSITE:
www.smett.mc

" Nadal's title in 2009 made him the first player ever to win an ATP World Tour Masters 1000 event five times in a row "

The Monte-Carlo Rolex Masters is widely regarded by players and fans alike as boasting the most picturesque backdrop to a centre court anywhere in the world – the stadium court at the Monte-Carlo Country Club overlooks the azure waters of the Mediterranean. The event is the first of three ATP World Tour Masters 1000s played on clay and is one of the longest-running tournaments in the world, dating back to 1897.

Over the years some of the game's great clay court masters have ruled in the principality, with Bjorn Borg, Thomas Muster, Gustavo Kuerten, Juan Carlos Ferrero and, of course, Rafael Nadal lifting the trophy since the early 1980s. No man has reigned supreme quite like Nadal, however, who has made the trophy his own in recent years, lifting the famous cup for the past five years, a tally one short of record-holding Englishman Reggie Doherty.

Nadal will be back in Monaco in 2010 with an incredible winning streak at the event stretching back over 27 matches. Nadal's three-set victory over Novak Djokovic in the 2009 final made him the first player ever to win an ATP World Tour Masters 1000 event five times in a row.

PAST **CHAMPIONS**

YEAR	SINGLES	DOUBLES
2009	Rafael Nadal (ESP)	Daniel Nestor (CAN) & Nenad Zimonjic (SRB)
2008	Rafael Nadal (ESP)	Rafael Nadal (ESP) & Tommy Robredo (ESP)
2007	Rafael Nadal (ESP)	Bob Bryan (USA) & Mike Bryan (USA)
2006	Rafael Nadal (ESP)	Jones Bjorkman (SWE) & Max Mirnyi (BLR)
2005	Rafael Nadal (ESP)	Leander Paes (IND) & Nenad Zimonjic (SRB)
2004	Guillermo Coria (ARG)	Tim Henman (GBR) & Nenad Zimonjic (SRB)
2003	Juan Carlos Ferrero (ESP)	Mahesh Bhupathi (IND) & Max Mirnyi (BLR)
2002	Juan Carlos Ferrero (ESP)	Jonas Bjorkman (SWE) & Todd Woodbridge (AUS)
2001	Gustavo Kuerten (BRA)	Jonas Bjorkman (SWE) & Todd Woodbridge (AUS)
2000	Cedric Pioline (FRA)	Wayne Ferreira (RSA) & Yevgeny Kafelnikov (RUS)

(L-R) DANIEL NESTOR & NENAD ZIMONJIC

APRIL 19-25 | BARCELONA, SPAIN

BARCELONA OPEN BANCO SABADELL

Barcelona
Open BancoSabadell
57 Trofeo Conde de Godó

500
ATP
WORLD TOUR

TOURNAMENT WEBSITE:
www.barcelonaopenbancosabadell.com

Draw: Singles-56 Doubles-24
Prize money: €1,550,000
Surface: Clay
Venue: Real Club de Tenis Barcelona 1899
Tournament director: Albert Costa
First held: 1953

One of the longest running and most important tournaments in Spain, this ATP World Tour 500 clay court event has been ruled by home grown players in recent years. Spaniards have lifted the famous trophy eight times in the last nine years and one man, Rafael Nadal, has become almost impossible to beat in Barcelona having won the title for the last five years.

The former world No.1 and six-time Grand Slam champion made it a high five by beating fellow Spaniard David Ferrer in the 2009 final, the same man he beat to claim the title 12 months earlier. "To win again here in Barcelona, in my home club and at such an important tournament is incredible," Nadal said.

The event is held on the red clay of the historic Real Club de Tenis Barcelona-1899, the oldest tennis club in Spain and one with a rich heritage since it has produced world class players such as Arantxa Sánchez-Vicario, Conchita Martínez, Carlos Moya and Albert Costa, who is now the tournament director.

RAFAEL NADAL

RAFAEL NADAL

PAST CHAMPIONS

(L-R) DANIEL NESTOR & NENAD ZIMONJIC

YEAR	SINGLES	DOUBLES
2009	Rafael Nadal (ESP)	Daniel Nestor (CAN) & Nenad Zimonjic (SRB)
2008	Rafael Nadal (ESP)	Bob Bryan (USA) & Mike Bryan (USA)
2007	Rafael Nadal (ESP)	Andrei Pavel (ROM) & Alexander Waske (GER)
2006	Rafael Nadal (ESP)	Mark Knowles (BAH) & Daniel Nestor (CAN)
2005	Rafael Nadal (ESP)	Leander Paes (IND) & Nenad Zimonjic (SRB)
2004	Tommy Robredo (ESP)	Mark Knowles (BAH) & Daniel Nestor (CAN)
2003	Carlos Moya (ESP)	Bob Bryan (USA) & Mike Bryan (USA)
2002	Gaston Gaudio (ARG)	Michael Hill (AUS) & Daniel Vacek (CZE)
2001	Juan Carlos Ferrero (ESP)	Donald Johnson (USA) & Jared Palmer (USA)
2000	Marat Safin (RUS)	Nicklas Kulti (SWE) & Mikael Tillstrom (SWE)

ATP WORLD TOUR
FEEL IT. WEAR IT.

www.ATPWorldTourStore.com

ONE TOUR. ONE STORE.

YOUR ON-LINE SOURCE FOR ATP WORLD TOUR OFFICIAL LICENCED PRODUCTS

www.ATPWorldTourStore.com

APRIL 25-MAY 2 | ROME, ITALY

INTERNAZIONALI BNL D'ITALIA

RAFAEL NADAL

©Julian Finney/Getty Images

Draw: Singles-56 Doubles-24
Prize money: €2,227,500
Surface: Clay
Venue: Foro Italico
Tournament director: Sergio Palmieri
First held: 1930

TOURNAMENT WEBSITE:
www.internazionalibnlditalia.it

" Rome's tennis fans flock to this glamorous tournament – its attendance figures have grown for the last six years "

The Internazionali BNL D'Italia is the second clay court ATP World Tour Masters 1000 of the year, sandwiched between Monte-Carlo and Madrid, and is another European event with a long history and rich heritage. The atmospheric and impressive Foro Italico is home to this glamorous event, a multi-sporting venue that hosted the 1960 summer Olympic Games and, as well as the tennis facilities, boasts the enormous Stadio Olimpico, the Stadio dei Marmi and the Stadio del Nuoto.

Ilie Nastase, Bjorn Borg, Vitas Gerulaitis, Andres Gomez, Ivan Lendl and Jim Courier all won the title twice, former Austrian world No.1 Thomas Muster captured a hat-trick of trophies, but it is Spain's Rafael Nadal who has enjoyed the most success having claimed the title four times in the last five years. In 2009 the Spaniard reclaimed the crown when he beat defending champion Novak Djokovic in straight sets in the final.

Every spring, Rome's tennis fans flock to this tournament – its attendance figures have grown year-on-year since 2004. Visitors enjoy mixing world class action with fine Italian food and great shopping, and in 2010 will be able to benefit from improved facilities following investment in the Foro Italico venue.

PAST **CHAMPIONS**

YEAR	SINGLES	DOUBLES
2009	Rafael Nadal (ESP)	Daniel Nestor (CAN) & Nenad Zimonjic (SRB)
2008	Novak Djokovic (SRB)	Bob Bryan (USA) & Mike Bryan (USA)
2007	Rafael Nadal (ESP)	Fabrice Santoro (FRA) & Nenad Zimonjic (SRB)
2006	Rafael Nadal (ESP)	Mark Knowles (BAH) & Daniel Nestor (CAN)
2005	Rafael Nadal (ESP)	Michael Llodra (FRA) & Fabrice Santoro (FRA)
2004	Carlos Moya (ESP)	Mahesh Bhupathi (IND) & Max Mirnyi (BLR)
2003	Felix Mantilla (ESP)	Wayne Arthurs (AUS) & Paul Hanley (AUS)
2002	Andre Agassi (USA)	Martin Damm (CZE) & Cyril Suk (CZE)
2001	Juan Carlos Ferrero (ESP)	Wayne Ferreira (RSA) & Yevgeny Kafelnikov (RUS)
2000	Magnus Norman (SWE)	Martin Damm (CZE) & Dominik Hrbaty (SVK)

(L-R) NENAD ZIMONJIC & DANIEL NESTOR

MAY 3-9 | ESTORIL, PORTUGAL

ESTORIL OPEN

TOURNAMENT WEBSITE:
www.estorilopen.net

Draw: Singles-28, Doubles-16
Prize money: €398,250
Surface: Clay
Venue: Estadio Nacional
Tournament director: João Lagos
First held: 1990

Such is the quality of the Estoril Open's field each May that seven different former French Open champions have won the Portuguese clay court title since the tournament was first played in 1990. Spaniards Sergi Bruguera, Albert Costa, Carlos Moya and Juan Carlos Ferrero, Austrian Thomas Muster, Argentine Gaston Gaudio and Swiss Roger Federer have all won in Estoril and Paris. In 2009 it was the turn of another Spaniard, Albert Montanes, to lift the trophy after he survived two match points before going on to beat American James Blake in the final. It wasn't the first incredible escape act Montanes had pulled off during the week – he saved a match point in the quarter-finals against top-seeded Frenchman Gilles Simon as well.

ALBERT MONTANES

PAST CHAMPIONS

YEAR	SINGLES	DOUBLES
2009	**Albert Montanes** (ESP)	**Eric Butorac** (USA) **& Scott Lipsky** (USA)
2008	**Roger Federer** (SUI)	**Jeff Coetzee** (RSA) **& Wesley Moodie** (RSA)
2007	**Novak Djokovic** (SRB)	**Marcelo Melo** (BRA) **& Andre Sa** (BRA)
2006	**David Nalbandian** (ARG)	**Lukas Dlouhy** (CZE) **& Pavel Vizner** (CZE)
2005	**Gaston Gaudio** (ARG)	**Frantisek Cermak** (CZE) **& Leos Friedl** (ARG)

MAY 3-9 | BELGRADE, SERBIA

SERBIA OPEN

TOURNAMENT WEBSITE:
www.serbiaopen.rs

Draw: Singles-28, Doubles-16
Prize money: €373,200
Surface: Clay
Venue: MGM, Belgrade
Tournament director: Goran Djokovic
First held: 2009

In 2009 the ATP World Tour went to Serbia for the first time ever when the inaugural clay court Serbia Open was staged in the country's capital Belgrade. Rather appropriately, former Grand Slam champion and local hero Novak Djokovic gave the local fans exactly what they wanted – a home-grown champion – when he ended the run of lucky loser Lukasz Kubot from Poland in the first ever final to come away with a 63 76(0) victory. The tournament was a huge success from the first ball struck to the last, and the 50,000-plus fans who poured through the gates in 2009 will be looking forward to the game's biggest stars returning to compete on Serbian soil for the second time in May 2010.

LUKASZ KUBOT

NOVAK DJOKOVIC

PAST CHAMPIONS

YEAR	SINGLES	DOUBLES
2009	**Novak Djokovic** (SRB)	**Lukasz Kubot** (POL) **& Oliver Marach** (AUT)

TICKET INFO: Call +49-89-54818181 or visit www.bmwopen.de

MAY 2-9 | MUNICH, GERMANY

BMW OPEN

TOURNAMENT WEBSITE:
www.bmwopen.de

Draw: Singles-32 Doubles-16
Prize money: €398,250
Surface: Clay
Venue: MTTC IPHITOS
Tournament director: Patrik Kuhnen
First held: 1990

TOMAS BERDYCH

The International Tennis Championships of Bavaria was first held in 1900, but the BMW Open, as it is now known, a clay court ATP World Tour 250 held during the countdown to the French Open, first came to Munich's Iphitos Tennis Club in 1974. The first of five ATP World Tour events held in Germany throughout the year, both BMW Open trophies went to Czech players in 2009. Tomas Berdych left with the singles silverware when he beat Russian Mikhail Youzhny in a dramatic three-set final, while the doubles title was won by Jan Hernych and Ivo Minar. Berdych will have been proud to add his name to an illustrious list of former winners, a roll of honour that includes Roger Federer, Nikolay Davydenko, David Nalbandian, Fernando Gonzalez, Michael Stich and Ivan Lendl.

PAST CHAMPIONS

YEAR	SINGLES	DOUBLES
2009	Tomas Berdych (CZE)	Jan Hernych (CZE) & Ivo Minar (CZE)
2008	Fernando Gonzalez (CHI)	Michael Berrer (GER) & Rainer Schuettler (GER)
2007	Philipp Kohlschreiber (GER)	Philipp Kohlschreiber (GER) & Mikhail Youzhny (RUS)
2006	Olivier Rochus (BEL)	Andrei Pavel (ROM) & Alexander Waske (GER)
2005	David Nalbandian (ARG)	Mario Ancic (CRO) & Julian Knowle (AUT)

NUMBER CRUNCHING

TOP 20 ALL-TIME OPEN ERA DOUBLES TITLE LEADERS

* Includes ATP World Tour, Grand Prix, WCT, Grand Slam, Grand Slam Cup

1	Todd Woodbridge (AUS)	83
=2	Tom Okker (NED)	78
	John McEnroe (USA)	78
4	Frew McMillan (RSA)	74
5	Mark Woodforde (AUS)	67
6	Peter Fleming (USA)	66
7	Bob Hewitt (AUS)	65
8	Daniel Nestor (CAN)	64
9	Raul Ramirez (MEX)	62
10	Stan Smith (USA)	61
11	Marty Riessen (USA)	60
=12	Mike Bryan (USA)	58
	Anders Jarryd (SWE)	58
14	Bob Bryan (USA)	56
15	Tomas Smid (CZE)	55
=16	Jonas Bjorkman (SWE)	54
	Brian Gottfried (USA)	54
	Paul Haarhuis (NED)	54
	Sherwood Stewart (USA)	54
20	Mark Knowles (BAH)	52

TODD WOODBRIDGE

ATP WORLD TOUR
MASTERS 1000

MAY 9-16 | MADRID, SPAIN

MUTUA MADRILEÑA MADRID OPEN

" Fans were welcomed into the event's stunning new state-of-the-art home, the Caja Magica, for the first time in 2009 "

The Mutua Madrileña Madrid Open is now one of the biggest and most prestigious European springtime combined tournaments having settled into its relatively new earlier slot in the ATP World Tour calendar. The Madrid event was first held in 2002 as an indoor tournament which took place in the autumn, but was moved forward to mid-May and changed surfaces in 2009, becoming one of three ATP World Tour Masters 1000s played on outdoor clay courts.

Fans were welcomed into the tournament's brand new home in 2009, the state-of-the-art Magic Box venue, located around 15 minutes south west of the city. Designed by Frenchman Dominique Perrault, the facility boasts three show courts, each with a retractable roof allowing play in all weather, four match courts in total and a further nine practice courts, all set within a fan-friendly environment.

Six players have claimed the title once since American Andre Agassi won the inaugural staging of the event in 2002, but Roger Federer set himself apart from the crowd last year when he collected his second Madrid title in four years. The Swiss beat home favourite Rafael Nadal in the final, ending the Spaniard's 33-match winning streak on clay.

PAST **CHAMPIONS**

YEAR	SINGLES	DOUBLES
2009	Roger Federer (SUI)	Daniel Nestor (CAN) & Nenad Zimonjic (SRB)
2008	Andy Murray (GBR)	Mariusz Fyrstenberg (POL) & Marcin Matkowski (POL)
2007	David Nalbandian (ARG)	Bob Bryan (USA) & Mike Bryan (USA)
2006	Roger Federer (SUI)	Bob Bryan (USA) & Mike Bryan (USA)
2005	Rafael Nadal (ESP)	Mark Knowles (BAH) & Daniel Nestor (CAN)
2004	Marat Safin (RUS)	Mark Knowles (BAH) & Daniel Nestor (CAN)
2003	Juan Carlos Ferrero (ESP)	Mahesh Bhupathi (IND) & Max Mirnyi (BLR)
2002	Andre Agassi (USA)	Mark Knowles (BAH) & Daniel Nestor (CAN)

(L-R) DANIEL NESTOR & NENAD ZIMONJIC

Draw: Singles-56 Doubles-24
Prize money: €2,835,000
Surface: Clay
Venue: Caja Mágica
Tournament director: Manolo Santana
First held: 2002

Sony Ericsson
WTA TOUR

MUTUAMADRILEÑA
MADRID OPEN

MASTERS
1000
ATP
WORLD TOUR

TOURNAMENT WEBSITE:
www.madrid-open.com

ROGER FEDERER

MAY 16-22 | NICE, FRANCE

OPEN DE NICE CÔTE D'AZUR

TOURNAMENT WEBSITE:
www.opennicecotedazur.com

ATP WORLD TOUR 250

Draw: Singles-28, Doubles-16
Prize money: €398,250
Surface: Clay
Venue: Nice Lawn Tennis Club
Tournament director:
Jean-François Caujolle
First held: 2010

The ATP World Tour returns to the cosmopolitan and glamorous city of Nice in 2010 following the relocation of the Interwetten Austrian Open from Kitzbühel to the south coast of France. The city hosted an ATP World Tour event for several years until 1995 with legends such as Ilie Nastase, Björn Borg, and Henri Leconte all tasting success over the years. The ATP World Tour 250 tournament will take place the week before Roland Garros on the 18 clay courts of the Nice Lawn Tennis Club, a venue that hosted a Fed Cup tie between France and Belgium in 1997. The tournament is one of five ATP World Tour events to be staged in France throughout the year and will offer €72,150 and 250 ranking points to its very first singles champion.

NUMBER CRUNCHING

TOTAL WEEKS AT NO.1 IN THE SOUTH AFRICAN AIRWAYS ATP RANKINGS

* Includes week of 28 December 2009

PLAYER	WEEKS AT NO.1
Pete Sampras (USA)	286
Ivan Lendl (CZE)	270
Jimmy Connors (USA)	268
Roger Federer (SUI)	*263
John McEnroe (USA)	170
Bjorn Borg (SWE)	109
Andre Agassi (USA)	101
Lleyton Hewitt (AUS)	80
Stefan Edberg (SWE)	72
Jim Courier (USA)	58
Rafael Nadal (ESP)	46
Gustavo Kuerten (BRA)	43
Ilie Nastase (ROM)	40
Mats Wilander (SWE)	20
Andy Roddick (USA)	13
Boris Becker (GER)	12
Marat Safin (RUS)	9
Juan Carlos Ferrero (ESP)	8
John Newcombe (AUS)	8
Yevgeny Kafelnikov (RUS)	6
Thomas Muster (AUT)	6
Marcelo Rios (CHI)	6
Carlos Moya (ESP)	2
Patrick Rafter (AUS)	1

PETE SAMPRAS

MAY 16-22 | DÜSSELDORF, GERMANY

ARAG ATP WORLD TEAM CHAMPIONSHIP

TOURNAMENT WEBSITE:
www.arag-world-team-cup.com

EIGHT-TEAM EVENT

Prize money: €1,351,000
Surface: Clay
Venue: Rochusclub
Tournament director: Dietloff von Arnim
First held: 1978

Some of the world's best players assemble in the water-side city of Düsseldorf every May to represent their countries in the ARAG ATP World Team Championship, a clay-court team event that takes place the week before Roland Garros. The event features eight teams and qualification is determined by taking the seven countries with the lowest aggregate ATP Rankings position of their top two players on December 7, 2009. One wild card team also gains direct entry into the tournament.

The teams are split into two groups of four with countries competing in a round robin format to decide the two group winners who face off in Saturday's final. Each tie consists of two singles matches and one doubles, all played in the relaxing surroundings of Düsseldorf's Rochusclub. The 2009 title went to Serbia, who edged out hosts Germany in the final. Viktor Troicki and Janko Tipsarevic led the Serbs to victory with singles successes against Rainer Schuettler and Philipp Kohlschreiber respectively. It was the first time Serbia had won the event since it first began in 1978.

When the qualification calculations for the 2010 event were made in November 2009, the seven teams guaranteed a spot in this year's tournament were Spain, Switzerland, France, Russia, Serbia, USA and the Czech Republic.

VIKTOR TROICKI

PAST **CHAMPIONS**

YEAR	COUNTRY
2009	Serbia
2008	Sweden
2007	Argentina
2006	Croatia
2005	Germany
2004	Chile
2003	Chile
2002	Argentina
2001	Australia
2000	Slovak Republic
1999	Australia
1998	Germany
1997	Spain
1996	Switzerland
1995	Sweden
1994	Germany
1993	USA
1992	Spain
1991	Sweden
1990	Yugoslavia

ARAG WORLD TE

MAY 23-JUNE 6 | PARIS, FRANCE

ROLAND GARROS

©Pascal Le Segretain/AFP/Getty Images

> ❝ Bjorn Borg still holds the record for most titles won in the Open era having notched up six between 1974 and 1981 ❞

Roland Garros, the second Grand Slam of the year and the only played on clay, was the first of the four majors to join the 'Open' era in 1968, and since then some of the biggest names in the world have raised the famous Coupe des Mousquetaires as men's singles champion. Sweden's Bjorn Borg still holds the record for most titles in the Open era with six (1974, 75, 78-81), while Gustavo Kuerten, Mats Wilander and Ivan Lendl all claimed a hat-trick of titles on Court Philippe Chatrier over the years.

In second place in the singles titles won standings is Rafael Nadal, who sensationally notched up four successive trophies between 2005 and 2008 before his shock defeat to Sweden's Robin Soderling in the fourth round in 2009, a result that ended a run of 31 victories for the Spaniard on the Paris clay.

And so it was the turn of Roger Federer to finally get his hands on the trophy after the heartbreak of finishing runner-up to Nadal three years in a row. His victory over Soderling in the 2009 final made Federer only the sixth man in history to win all four Grand Slam singles titles. The result also saw him tie American Pete Sampras' all-time record of 14 major singles titles, a tally he went on to surpass at Wimbledon.

PAST **CHAMPIONS**

YEAR	SINGLES	DOUBLES
2009	Roger Federer (SUI)	Lukas Dlouhy (CZE) & Leander Paes (IND)
2008	Rafael Nadal (ESP)	Pablo Cuevas (URU) & Luis Horna (PER)
2007	Rafael Nadal (ESP)	Mark Knowles (BAH) Daniel Nestor (CAN)
2006	Rafael Nadal (ESP)	Jonas Bjorkman (SWE) & Max Mirnyi (BLR)
2005	Rafael Nadal (ESP)	Jonas Bjorkman (SWE) & Max Mirnyi (BLR)
2004	Gaston Gaudio (ARG)	Xavier Malisse (BEL) & Olivier Rochus (BEL)
2003	Juan Carlos Ferrero (ESP)	Bob Bryan (USA) & Mike Bryan (USA)
2002	Albert Costa (ESP)	Paul Haarhuis (NED) & Yevgeny Kafelnikov (RUS)
2001	Gustavo Kuerten (BRA)	Mahesh Bhupathi (IND) & Leander Paes (IND)
2000	Gustavo Kuerten (BRA)	Todd Woodbridge (AUS) & Mark Woodforde (AUS)

(L-R) LUKAS DLOUHY & LEANDER PAES

©Matthew Stockman/Getty Images

Draw: Singles-128 Doubles-64
Prize money: TBD
Surface: Clay
Venue: Roland Garros
Tournament director:
Sandra de Jenken Eversmann
First held: 1891

GRAND SLAM®
(2000 POINTS)

TOURNAMENT WEBSITE:
www.rolandgarros.com

ROGER FEDERER

JUNE 7-13 | HALLE, GERMANY

GERRY WEBER OPEN

TOURNAMENT WEBSITE:
www.gerryweber-open.de

Draw: Singles-32, Doubles-16
Prize money: €663,750
Surface: Grass
Venue: Gerry Weber Stadion
Tournament director: Ralf Weber
First held: 1993

With the red dust settling on the European clay court season, the brief grass court swing begins in Europe with ATP World Tour 250s in London and in Halle at the Gerry Weber Open. The German tournament is one of just five grass court get-togethers on the ATP World Tour calendar and has been dominated by one of the most formidable players on the surface in recent years – Roger Federer. The Swiss star has often used the Halle event to fine-tune his Wimbledon preparations and has won the event four times. German wild card Tommy Haas gave the home fans plenty to cheer in 2009, however, when he shocked Serbia's Novak Djokovic to claim the trophy before going on reach the semi-finals at Wimbledon two weeks later.

TOMMY HAAS

©Lars Baron/Bongarts/Getty Images

PAST CHAMPIONS

YEAR	SINGLES	DOUBLES
2009	Tommy Haas (GER)	Christopher Kas (GER) & Philipp Kohlschreiber (GER)
2008	Roger Federer (SUI)	Mikhail Youzhny (RUS) & Mischa Zverev (GER)
2007	Tomas Berdych (CZE)	Simon Aspelin (SWE) & Julian Knowle (AUT)
2006	Roger Federer (SUI)	Fabrice Santoro (FRA) & Nenad Zimonjic (SRB)
2005	Roger Federer (SUI)	Yves Allegro (SUI) & Roger Federer (SUI)

JUNE 7-13 | LONDON, ENGLAND

AEGON CHAMPIONSHIPS

TOURNAMENT WEBSITE:
www.aegonchampionships.com

Draw: Singles-56, Doubles-16
Prize money: €627,700
Surface: Grass
Venue: The Queen's Club
Tournament director: Chris Kermode
First held: 1979

Such is its importance in the grass court calendar that since its birth in 1979, 25 of the past 27 Wimbledon champions have played at the AEGON Championships, held in the perfect settings of the Queen's Club in west London. Some of the true greats of grass court tennis have used the event as the perfect environment to put the finishing touches to their Wimbledon preparations and the likes of John McEnroe, Jimmy Connors, Ivan Lendl, Boris Becker, Stefan Edberg, Pete Sampras, Rafael Nadal, Lleyton Hewitt and Andy Roddick have all held aloft the famous, gigantic trophy over the years. In 2009 Andy Murray captured his first ATP World Tour title on home soil to become the first British winner at Queen's since Bunny Austin in 1938.

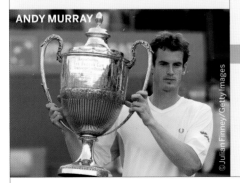

ANDY MURRAY

©Julian Finney/Getty Images

PAST CHAMPIONS

YEAR	SINGLES	DOUBLES
2009	Andy Murray (GBR)	Wesley Moodie (RSA) & Mikhail Youzhny (RUS)
2008	Rafael Nadal (ESP)	Daniel Nestor (CAN) & Nenad Zimonjic (SRB)
2007	Andy Roddick (USA)	Mark Knowles (BAH) & Daniel Nestor (CAN)
2006	Lleyton Hewitt (AUS)	Paul Hanley (AUS) & Kevin Ullyett (ZIM)
2005	Andy Roddick (USA)	Bob Bryan (USA) & Mike Bryan (USA)

JUNE 13-19 | S'-HERTONGENBOSCH, THE NETHERLANDS

ORDINA OPEN

Sony Ericsson
WTA TOUR

250
ATP
WORLD TOUR

TOURNAMENT WEBSITE:
www.ordina-open.nl

Draw:	Singles-32 Doubles-16
Prize money:	€398,250
Surface:	Grass
Venue:	Autotron Rosmalen
Tournament director:	Marcel Hunze
First held:	1990

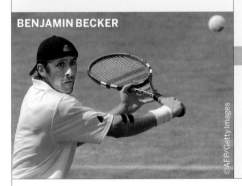

BENJAMIN BECKER

The second week of the short, sharp grass court swing sees ATP World Tour action move to The Netherlands with stars from the men's and women's tours assembling in s'-Hertongenbosch for a combined grass court tournament, the Ordina Open. Goran Ivanisevic began the trend of Croatians winning big grass court titles when he won Wimbledon in 2001, and Ivan Ljubicic and Mario Ancic both proved Goran isn't the only player from their country who can play on the surface by winning in s'-Hertongenbosch between 2005 and 2007. In 2009 it was another familiar grass court name who ruled – Becker – but this time the surname belonged to young German, Benjamin, who claimed his first ever ATP World Tour title when he beat Dutch wild card Raemon Sluiter in the final.

PAST CHAMPIONS

YEAR	SINGLES	DOUBLES
2009	Benjamin Becker (GER)	Wesley Moodie (RSA) & Dick Norman (BEL)
2008	David Ferrer (ESP)	Mario Ancic (CRO) & Jurgen Melzer (AUT)
2007	Ivan Ljubicic (CRO)	Jeff Coetzee (RSA) & Rogier Wassen (NED)
2006	Mario Ancic (CRO)	Martin Damm (CZE) & Leander Paes (IND)
2005	Mario Ancic (CRO)	Cyril Suk (CZE) & Pavel Vizner (CZE)

JUNE 13-19 | EASTBOURNE, ENGLAND

AEGON INTERNATIONAL

Sony Ericsson
WTA TOUR

AEGON
INTERNATIONAL

250
ATP
WORLD TOUR

TOURNAMENT WEBSITE: wwww.lta.org.uk/
Watch/AEGON-British-Tennis-Series/AEGON-International/

Draw:	Singles-32, Doubles-16
Prize money:	€405,000
Surface:	Grass
Venue:	Devonshire Park
Tournament director:	Gavin Fletcher
First held:	1996

DMITRY TURSUNOV

Formerly the International Women's Open, Britain's biggest international women's event joined forces with the ATP World Tour in 2009 to host a combined men's and women's tournament in the perfect surroundings of Eastbourne's Devonshire Park, on England's so-called 'Sunshine Coast'. Before moving to Eastbourne, the men's ATP World Tour event was played in Nottingham the week before Wimbledon, where Ivo Karlovic won back-to-back titles in 2007 and 2008 and Frenchman Richard Gasquet claimed consecutive crowns in 2005 and 2006. In 2009 Russian Dmitry Tursunov became the first male champion at Devonshire Park when he beat Canadian qualifier Frank Dancevic in the final. It was Tursunov's sixth ATP World Tour title and his first on grass.

PAST CHAMPIONS

YEAR	SINGLES	DOUBLES
2009	Dmitry Tursunov (RUS)	Mariusz Fyrstenberg (POL) & Marcin Matkowski (POL)
2008	Ivo Karlovic (CRO)	Bruno Soares (BRA) & Kevin Ullyett (ZIM)
2007	Ivo Karlovic (CRO)	Eric Butorac (USA) & Jamie Murray (GBR)
2006	Richard Gasquet (FRA)	Jonathan Erlich (ISR) & Andy Ram (ISR)
2005	Richard Gasquet (FRA)	Jonathan Erlich (ISR) & Andy Ram (ISR)

JUNE 21-JULY 4 | LONDON, ENGLAND

WIMBLEDON

GRAND SLAM
2000 POINTS

ROGER FEDERER

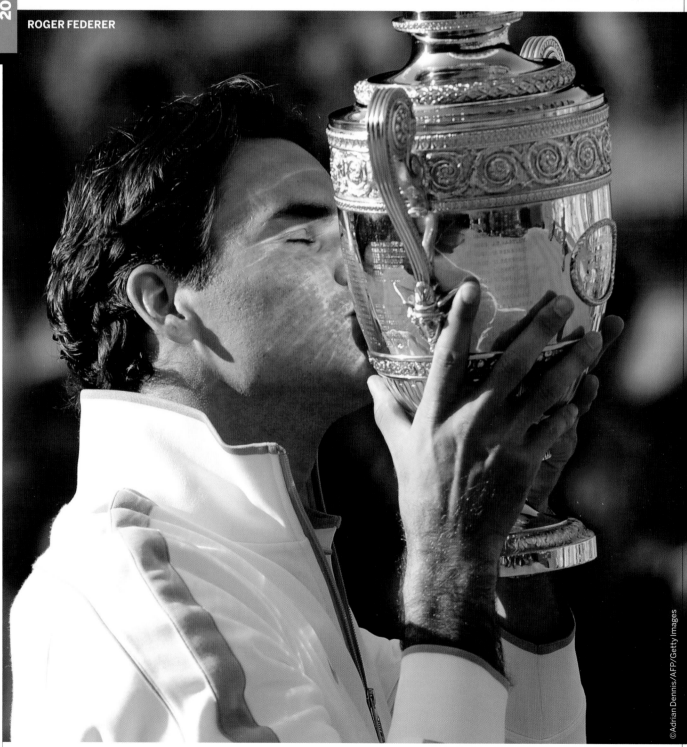

©Adrian Dennis/AFP/Getty Images

Draw: Singles-128 Doubles-64
Prize money: TBD
Surface: Grass
Venue: All England Club
Tournament director: Ian Ritchie
First held: 1877

GRAND SLAM®
(2000 POINTS)

TOURNAMENT WEBSITE:
www.wimbledon.org

" Federer is second behind Sampras in titles won during the Open era. Sampras ruled SW19 seven times in eight years "

The Championships, now well over 100 years old, is steeped in tradition. Every June the All England Club opens its gates to the best men and women who battle it out on the immaculate 15,000-capacity Centre Court and numerous pristine 'outside' courts to be crowned Wimbledon champion.

In recent years Swiss Roger Federer has made the event his own, collecting six men's singles titles in seven years to put himself in second place behind Pete Sampras' seven trophies in the singles titles won during the Open era leaderboard. Sampras held the famous golden trophy aloft seven times in eight years between 1993 and 2000.

The 2009 Championships will be remembered for two things – the new retractable Centre Court roof which allowed play to continue in wet weather and one of the greatest men's singles finals of all time.

On the final Sunday Federer outlasted American Andy Roddick over five sets, the Swiss emerging with a 57 76(6) 76(5) 36 1614 victory in a match that lasted four hours and 16 minutes and featured the longest deciding set in Grand Slam final history. The hard-fought victory also earned Federer a record-breaking 15th Grand Slam singles title, one more than Sampras.

WIMBLEDON CENTRE COURT

PAST **CHAMPIONS**

YEAR	SINGLES	DOUBLES
2009	**Roger Federer** (SUI)	**Daniel Nestor** (CAN) & **Nenad Zimonjic** (SRB)
2008	**Rafael Nadal** (ESP)	**Daniel Nestor** (CAN) & **Nenad Zimonjic** (SRB)
2007	**Roger Federer** (SUI)	**Arnaud Clement** (FRA) & **Michael Llodra** (FRA)
2006	**Roger Federer** (SUI)	**Bob Bryan** (USA) & **Mike Bryan** (USA)
2005	**Roger Federer** (SUI)	**Stephen Huss** (AUS) & **Wes Moodie** (RSA)
2004	**Roger Federer** (SUI)	**Jonas Bjorkman** (SWE) & **Todd Woodbridge** (AUS)
2003	**Roger Federer** (SUI)	**Jonas Bjorkman** (SWE) & **Todd Woodbridge** (AUS)
2002	**Lleyton Hewitt** (AUS)	**Jonas Bjorkman** (SWE) & **Todd Woodbridge** (AUS)
2001	**Goran Ivanisevic** (CRO)	**Donald Johnson** (USA) & **Jared Palmer** (USA)
2000	**Pete Sampras** (USA)	**Todd Woodbridge** (AUS) & **Mark Woodforde** (AUS)

(L-R) DANIEL NESTOR & NENAD ZIMONJIC

JULY 5-11 | NEWPORT, RHODE ISLAND, USA

CAMPBELL'S HALL OF FAME TENNIS CHAMPIONSHIPS

TOURNAMENT WEBSITE:
www.tennisfame.com

Draw: Singles-32, Doubles-16
Prize money: $442,500
Surface: Grass
Venue: International Tennis Hall of Fame
Tournament director: Mark L. Stenning
First held: 1881

Visitors to the Campbell's Hall of Fame Tennis Championships, the final week of grass court tennis on the ATP World Tour calendar, will be able to watch some of the world's best amid truly historic surroundings. The ATP World Tour 250 event is held at the International Tennis Hall of Fame & Museum, on the same courts that hosted the first U.S. National Lawn Tennis Championship way back in 1881. As well as the tennis, visitors can enjoy the Hall of Fame complex and Museum which have been restored following a $7.5 million renovation project. American lucky loser Rajeev Ram captured his first ATP World Tour singles title when he beat countryman Sam Querrey in the 2009 final, before teaming up with Australian Jordan Kerr to win the doubles trophy as well.

PAST CHAMPIONS

YEAR	SINGLES	DOUBLES
2009	Rajeev Ram (USA)	Jordan Kerr (AUS) & Rajeev Ram (USA)
2008	Fabrice Santoro (FRA)	Mardy Fish (USA) & John Isner (USA)
2007	Fabrice Santoro (FRA)	Jordan Kerr (AUS) & Jim Thomas (USA)
2006	Mark Philippoussis (AUS)	Robert Kendrick (USA) & Jurgen Melzer (AUT)
2005	Greg Rusedski (GBR)	Jordan Kerr (AUS) & Jim Thomas (USA)

JULY 12-18 | BÅSTAD, SWEDEN

SKISTAR SWEDISH OPEN

TOURNAMENT WEBSITE:
www.swedishopen.org

Draw: Singles-28, Doubles-16
Prize money: €398,250
Surface: Clay
Venue: Båstad Tennis Stadium
Tournament director: Thomas Wallén
First held: 1947

Anyone who has visited the coastal town of Båstad, in south-west Sweden, will understand why its summer clay court tournament, the SkiStar Swedish Open, has been voted the ATP World Tour 250 Tournament of the Year for a record seven consecutive seasons. The organisers of this event, the first European summer clay court tournament on the calendar following the grass court swing, have consistently improved their venue and tournament. Swedish fans had the added bonus of cheering one of their own on to victory in 2009 when French Open runner-up Robin Soderling became the first Swedish winner since his coach Magnus Norman won the title in 2000. The powerful Swede didn't drop a set all week, seeing off Argentine Juan Monaco in style in the final.

ROBIN SODERLING

PAST CHAMPIONS

YEAR	SINGLES	DOUBLES
2009	Robin Soderling (SWE)	Jaroslav Levinsky (CZE) & Filip Polasek (SVK)
2008	Tommy Robredo (ESP)	Jonas Bjorkman (SWE) & Robin Soderling (SWE)
2007	David Ferrer (ESP)	Simon Aspelin (SWE) & Julian Knowle (AUT)
2006	Tommy Robredo (ESP)	Jonas Bjorkman (SWE) & Thomas Johansson (SWE)
2005	Rafael Nadal (ESP)	Jonas Bjorkman (SWE) & Joachim Johansson (SWE)

JULY 12-18 | STUTTGART, GERMANY

MERCEDESCUP

MercedesCup

TOURNAMENT WEBSITE:
www.mercedescup.de

Draw:	Singles-28 Doubles-16
Prize money:	€398,250
Surface:	Clay
Venue:	TC Weissenhof
Tournament director:	Edwin Weindorfer
First held:	1886

The MercedesCup, along with an ATP World Tour 250 held in Sweden the same week, kick-starts a three-week European summer clay court swing. Players that favour the 'dirt', as it's known, are often keen to return to the surface following the grass court season and the likes of Rafael Nadal, Juan Martin Del Potro, Gustavo Kuerten and Thomas Muster have all won in the German city. In 2009 the event witnessed a brand new ATP World Tour title winner when Frenchman Jeremy Chardy claimed the first singles trophy of his career when he took down Victor Hanescu in three sets. The result made Chardy the first French winner of the event since Henri Leconte in 1984 and the new champion had the added bonus of driving away in a brand new Mercedes E350, a gift from the title sponsors.

PAST **CHAMPIONS**

YEAR	SINGLES	DOUBLES
2009	Jeremy Chardy (FRA)	Frantisek Cermak (CZE) & Michal Mertinak (SVK)
2008	Juan Martin Del Potro (ARG)	Christopher Kas (GER) & Philipp Kohlschreiber (GER)
2007	Rafael Nadal (ESP)	Frantisek Cermak (CZE) & Leos Friedl (CZE)
2006	David Ferrer (ESP)	Gaston Gaudio (ARG) & Max Mirnyi (BLR)
2005	Rafael Nadal (ESP)	Jose Acasuso (ARG) & Sebastian Prieto (ARG)

JULY 19-25 | ATLANTA, GEORGIA, USA

ATLANTA TENNIS CHAMPIONSHIPS

TOURNAMENT WEBSITE:
www.atlantatennischampionships.com

Draw:	Singles-32, Doubles-16
Prize money:	$531,000
Surface:	Hard
Venue:	TBD
Tournament director:	Bill Oakes
First held:	2010

The city of Atlanta, Georgia, will welcome stars of the ATP World Tour once again in 2010 for the first time since 2001. The southern city, which hosted the 1996 Olympic Games, last staged an ATP World Tour event between 1992 and 2001 on green clay. American Andy Roddick won his first ATP World Tour title in Atlanta in 2001. The tournament will offer over half a million dollars in prize money and is the first event in the Olympus US Open Series which groups ten American hard court tournaments leading up to the US Open at the end of August. The 2009 series set a new record with nearly 47 million viewers across the six-week season – the largest TV audience in its six-year history.

JULY 19-25 | HAMBURG, GERMANY

INTERNATIONAL GERMAN OPEN HAMBURG

international **GERMAN OPEN**

TOURNAMENT WEBSITE: www.amrothenbaum.de

Draw: Singles-48 Doubles-16
Prize money: €1,100,000
Surface: Clay
Venue: Rothenbaum Sport GmbH
Tournament director: Michael Stich
First held: 1897

Germany's tennis fans get the chance to enjoy some high-quality competition every summer when the impressive Rothenbaum Tennis Center welcomes 48 of the world's best players for the clay court International German Open Hamburg. The prestigious event dates way back to 1897 and many of the sport's most accomplished clay courters have held the trophy aloft inside the Rothenbaum's 13,200-seat centre court stadium over the years. In the past decade Swiss superstar Roger Federer has won four times, and has been joined on the roll of honour by Spanish clay court king Rafael Nadal, Argentina's Guillermo Coria and former world No.1 Gustavo Kuerten from Brazil. In 2009 it was Nikolay Davydenko who ended the week as champion when he beat Frenchman Paul-Henri Mathieu in an entertaining final, a result that seemed to kick-start his year. The Russian went on to win another trophy seven days later in Croatia and ultimately claimed five titles, including the season-ending Barclays ATP World Tour Finals, in the second half of the season.

NIKOLAY DAVYDENKO

©Martin Rose/Bongarts/Getty Images

©Stuart Franklin/Bongarts/Getty Images

©Martin Rose/Bongarts/Getty Images

PAST **CHAMPIONS**

YEAR	SINGLES	DOUBLES
2009	**Nikolay Davydenko** (RUS)	**Simon Aspelin** (SWE) **& Paul Hanley** (AUS)
2008	**Rafael Nadal** (ESP)	**Daniel Nestor** (CAN) **& Nenad Zimonjic** (SRB)
2007	**Roger Federer** (SUI)	**Bob Bryan** (USA) **& Mike Bryan** (USA)
2006	**Tommy Robredo** (ESP)	**Paul Hanley** (AUS) **& Kevin Ullyett** (ZIM)
2005	**Roger Federer** (SUI)	**Jonas Bjorkman** (SWE) **& Max Mirnyi** (BLR)
2004	**Roger Federer** (SUI)	**Wayne Black** (ZIM) **& Kevin Ullyett** (ZIM)
2003	**Guillermo Coria** (ARG)	**Mark Knowles** (BAH) **& Daniel Nestor** (CAN)
2002	**Roger Federer** (SUI)	**Mahesh Bhupathi** (IND) **& Jan-Michael Gambill** (USA)
2001	**Albert Portas** (ESP)	**Jonas Bjorkman** (SWE) **& Todd Woodbridge** (AUS)
2000	**Gustavo Kuerten** (BRA)	**Todd Woodbridge** (AUS) **& Mark Woodforde** (AUS)

JULY 25-AUGUST 1 | GSTAAD, SWITZERLAND

ALLIANZ SUISSE OPEN

ALLIANZ SUISSE OPEN
GSTAAD PRESENTED BY MONDOBIOTECH
24 JULY - 1ST AUGUST 2010

TOURNAMENT WEBSITE:
www.allianzsuisseopengstaad.com

Draw: Singles-32 Doubles-16
Prize money: €398,250
Surface: Clay
Venue: Roy Emerson Arena
Tournament director: Jean-François Collet
First held: 1915

There are few tournaments on the ATP World Tour that can boast such dramatic mountain scenery as a backdrop, the kind of natural beauty that makes the Allianz Suisse Open in Gstaad one of the most picturesque stops on the calendar. As well as the scenery, the tournament will also be remembered by many as the venue where Swiss hero Roger Federer (who captured the title in 2004) was presented with a cow in a homecoming ceremony shortly after winning his first Wimbledon title. Brazilian qualifier Thomaz Bellucci beat all before him in 2009 to claim his first ever ATP World Tour title, seeing off German Andreas Beck in the final. The result made Bellucci the first Brazilian to win an ATP World Tour title for five years.

THOMAZ BELLUCCI

PAST CHAMPIONS

YEAR	SINGLES	DOUBLES
2009	Thomaz Bellucci (BRA)	Marco Chiudinelli (SUI) & Michael Lammer (SUI)
2008	Victor Hanescu (ROM)	Jaroslav Levinsky (CZE) & Filip Polasek (SVK)
2007	Paul-Henri Mathieu (FRA)	Frantisek Cermak (CZE) & Pavel Vizner (CZE)
2006	Richard Gasquet (FRA)	Jiri Novak (CZE) & Andrei Pavel (ROM)
2005	Gaston Gaudio (ARG)	Frantisek Cermak (CZE) & Leos Friedl (CZE)

JULY 26-AUGUST 1 | UMAG, CROATIA

CROATIA OPEN UMAG

TOURNAMENT WEBSITE:
www.croatiaopen.hr

Draw: Singles-28, Doubles-16
Prize money: €398,250
Surface: Clay
Venue: ITC Stella Maris
Tournament director: Vanja Bozickovic
First held: 1990

The Croatia Open Umag is another European clay court event that has attracted some of the world's best slow court specialists over the years since it was first held in 1990. Austrian former world No.1 Thomas Muster won the title three times in four years, another former world No.1, Spain's Carlos Moya, has lifted the trophy five times, including three straight between 2001 and 2003, while more recently Croatia's tennis fans have watched as Guillermo Coria, Stanislas Wawrinka, Fernando Verdasco and in 2009 Nikolay Davydenko were crowned champions. Slovakian Michal Mertinak should have particularly fond memories of the tournament, too, since he has won the doubles trophy for the last three years – each year with a different partner.

NIKOLAY DAVYDENKO

PAST CHAMPIONS

YEAR	SINGLES	DOUBLES
2009	Nikolay Davydenko (RUS)	Frantisek Cermak (CZE) & Michal Mertinak (SVK)
2008	Fernando Verdasco (ESP)	Michal Mertinak (SVK) & Petr Pala (CZE)
2007	Carlos Moya (ESP)	Lukas Dlouhy (CZE) & Michal Mertinak (SVK)
2006	Stanislas Wawrinka (SUI)	Jaroslav Levinsky (CZE) & David Skoch (CZE)
2005	Guillermo Coria (ARG)	Jiri Novak (CZE) & Petr Pala (CZE)

JULY 26-AUGUST 1 | LOS ANGELES, CA, USA

LA TENNIS OPEN
PRESENTED BY FARMERS INSURANCE GROUP

ATP WORLD TOUR 250

TOURNAMENT WEBSITE:
www.latennisopen.com

Draw: Singles-28, Doubles-16
Prize money: $619,500
Surface: Hard
Venue: Straus Stadium/
Los Angeles Tennis Center - UCLA
Tournament director: Bob Kramer
First held: 1927

The University of California Los Angeles (UCLA) hosts the city's longest running annual professional sporting event every July, welcoming some of the world's best to its first-class facilities. This ATP World Tour 250 hard court event is 83 years old and has had some true greats lift its trophy over the years. American Andre Agassi won the tournament four times, as did Jimmy Connors, and John McEnroe, Boris Becker, Stefan Edberg and Pete Sampras have all tasted victory in California. Sam Querrey made sure the trophy stayed on home soil in 2009 when he beat Australian qualifier Carsten Ball in his third successive final on the ATP World Tour. The LA event is also a favourite for the Bryan brothers who have won the doubles title five times in the last nine years.

SAM QUERREY

PAST **CHAMPIONS**

YEAR	SINGLES	DOUBLES
2009	Sam Querrey (USA)	Bob Bryan (USA) & Mike Bryan (USA)
2008	Juan Martin Del Potro (USA)	Rohan Bopanna (IND) & Eric Butorac (USA)
2007	Radek Stepanek (CZE)	Bob Bryan (USA) & Mike Bryan (USA)
2006	Tommy Haas (USA)	Bob Bryan (USA) & Mike Bryan (USA)
2005	Andre Agassi (USA)	Rick Leach (USA) & Brian MacPhie (USA)

NUMBER CRUNCHING

ARGENTINES IN YEAR-END TOP 10

In 2009, Juan Martin del Potro finished in the Top 10 for the second consecutive year and he is one of seven Argentines to rank in the year-end Top 10.

JUAN MARTIN DEL POTRO

GUILLERMO VILAS

	PLAYER	TOP 10 FINISHES	YEAR	BEST YEAR-END RANK	YEAR
1	Guillermo Vilas	9	(1974-82)	No. 2	(1975, '77)
2	David Nalbandian	5	(2003-07)	No. 6	(2005)
3	Jose-Luis Clerc	4	(1980-83)	No. 5	(1981)
4	Guillermo Coria	3	(2003-05)	No. 5	(2003)
=5	Juan Martin Del Potro	2	(2008-09)	No. 5	(2009)
	Gaston Gaudio	2	(2004-05)	No. 10	(2004-05)
7	Alberto Mancini	1	(1989)	No. 9	(1989)

>> **TICKET INFO:** Call +1 202 721 9500 or visit www.leggmasontennisclassic.com

AUGUST 1-8 | WASHINGTON DC, USA

LEGG MASON TENNIS CLASSIC

TOURNAMENT WEBSITE:
www.leggmasontennisclassic.com

Draw: Singles-48 Doubles-16
Prize money: $1,165,500
Surface: Hard
Venue: William H.G. Fitzgerald Tennis Center
Tournament director: Jeff Newman
First held: 1969

Washington DC has become a popular location for Argentine Juan Martin Del Potro after the so-called 'Tower of Tandil' claimed back-to-back titles at the William H.G. Fitzgerald Tennis Center in 2008 and 2009. His success at the event in 2008 came during a red-hot run of form that saw him collect four successive singles trophies and 12 months later he successfully defended his Washington crown, a result that gave the world a glimpse of the kind of tennis that would deliver his first Grand Slam crown a few weeks later in New York. Del Potro is one of a host of true greats of the game to have won the Legg Mason Tennis Classic, an event that dates back to 1969. In its early years the likes of Arthur Ashe, Jimmy Connors, Ivan Lendl and five-time champion Andre Agassi all reigned at the hard court tournament, while more recently its champions have included former world No.1s Lleyton Hewitt and three-time winner Andy Roddick, the man Del Potro beat to get his hands on the silverware in 2009.

THE WHITE HOUSE, WASHINGTON DC

JUAN MARTIN DEL POTRO

(L-R) MARTIN DAMM & ROBERT LINDSTEDT

PAST **CHAMPIONS**

YEAR	SINGLES	DOUBLES
2009	Juan Martin Del Potro (ARG)	Martin Damm (CZE) & Robert Lindstedt (SWE)
2008	Juan Martin Del Potro (ARG)	Marc Gicquel (FRA) & Robert Lindstedt (SWE)
2007	Andy Roddick (USA)	Bob Bryan (USA) & Mike Bryan (USA)
2006	Arnaud Clement (FRA)	Bob Bryan (USA) & Mike Bryan (USA)
2005	Andy Roddick (USA)	Bob Bryan (USA) & Mike Bryan (USA)
2004	Lleyton Hewitt (AUS)	Chris Haggard (RSA) & Robbie Koenig (RSA)
2003	Tim Henman (GBR)	Yevgeny Kafelnikov (RUS) & Sargis Sargsian (ARM)
2002	James Blake (USA)	Wayne Black (ZIM) & Kevin Ullyett (ZIM)
2001	Andy Roddick (USA)	Martin Damm (CZE) & David Prinosil (GER)
2000	Alex Corretja (ESP)	Alex O'Brien (USA) & Jared Palmer (USA)

AUGUST 9-15 | TORONTO, CANADA

ROGERS CUP

ATP WORLD TOUR
MASTERS 1000

ANDY MURRAY

©Julian Finney/Getty Images

Draw: Singles-56 Doubles-24
Prize money: $2,430,000
Surface: Hard
Venue: Rexall Centre
Tournament director: Karl Hale
First held: 1881

TOURNAMENT WEBSITE:
www.rogerscup.com

> The Canadian tournament was first held back in 1881 and is the oldest ongoing event after Wimbledon and the US Open

The Rogers Cup alternates between the Canadian cities of Toronto and Montreal every summer and is the oldest ongoing tennis tournament after Wimbledon and the US Open. The event was first held back in 1881 and is the first ATP World Tour Masters 1000 of the North American hard court swing which comes to a climax at the US Open in September.

Roger Federer, Rafael Nadal, Andy Roddick, Andre Agassi, John McEnroe, Boris Becker and Bjorn Borg have all held aloft the Canadian trophy over the years but none can match the achievements of former world No.1 Ivan Lendl who tasted glory an incredible six times in ten years between 1980-89, including a hat-trick of titles from 1987-89.

Andy Murray made history in 2009 when he finished as the last man standing when the tournament was held in Montreal, beating US Open champion-to-be Juan Martin Del Potro in the final for the fourth ATP World Tour Masters 1000 title of his career. The young Scot became the first British champion at the Canadian tournament and the victory pushed Murray up to No.2 in the South African Airways 2009 ATP Rankings, which made him the highest ever ranked British player.

PAST CHAMPIONS

YEAR	SINGLES	DOUBLES
2009	Andy Murray (GBR)	Mahesh Bhupathi (IND) & Mark Knowles (BAH)
2008	Rafael Nadal (ESP)	Daniel Nestor (CAN) & Nenad Zimonjic (SRB)
2007	Novak Djokovic (SRB)	Mahesh Bhupathi (IND) & Pavel Vizner (CZE)
2006	Roger Federer (SUI)	Bob Bryan (USA) & Mike Bryan (USA)
2005	Rafael Nadal (ESP)	Wayne Black (ZIM) & Kevin Ullyett (ZIM)
2004	Roger Federer (SUI)	Mahesh Bhupathi (IND) & Leander Paes (IND)
2003	Andy Roddick (USA)	Mahesh Bhupathi (IND) & Max Mirnyi (BLR)
2002	Guillermo Cañas (ARG)	Bob Bryan (USA) & Mike Bryan (USA)
2001	Andrei Pavel (ROM)	Jiri Novak (CZE) & David Rikl (CZE)
2000	Marat Safin (RUS)	Sebastien Lareau (CAN) & Daniel Nestor (CAN)

(L-R) MAHESH BHUPATHI & MARK KNOWLES

AUGUST 15-22 | CINCINNATI, OHIO, USA

WESTERN & SOUTHERN FINANCIAL GROUP MASTERS

" The quality of the field in Cincinnati is of the highest order – every champion from 2001-2007 held the world No.1 ranking "

The Western & Southern Financial Group Masters, the second of back-to-back hard court ATP World Tour Masters 1000s held in August, is a world class tournament with a world class heritage. The American event is one of the oldest on the ATP World Tour, first staged at the Avondale Athletic Club in 1899, and now held at the Lindner Family Tennis Center in Cincinnati, Ohio. The quality of the field each year is reflected in its list of recent champions – the seven champions preceding 2008 winner Andy Murray all held the No.1 ranking during their careers.

Swiss star Roger Federer collected his third Cincinnati title in 2009 when he beat Serbia's Novak Djokovic in the final, only the fourth player to have completed a hat-trick in Ohio. Sweden's former world No.1 Mats Wilander leads the pack with four titles between 1983 and 1988. The 2009 doubles final was particularly memorable when Daniel Nestor and Nenad Zimonjic saved an incredible eight match points in the deciding Match Tie-break to beat defending champions Bob Bryan and Mike Bryan 3-6, 7-6(2), 15-13 in one of the most dramatic doubles contests of the year.

PAST **CHAMPIONS**

YEAR	SINGLES	DOUBLES
2009	Roger Federer (SUI)	Daniel Nestor (CAN) & Nenad Zimonjic (SRB)
2008	Andy Murray (GBR)	Bob Bryan (USA) & Mike Bryan (USA)
2007	Roger Federer (SUI)	Jonathan Erlich (ISR) & Andy Ram (ISR)
2006	Andy Roddick (USA)	Jonas Bjorkman (SWE) & Max Mirnyi (BLR)
2005	Roger Federer (SUI)	Jonas Bjorkman (SWE) & Max Mirnyi (BLR)
2004	Andre Agassi (USA)	Mark Knowles (BAH) & Daniel Nestor (CAN)
2003	Andy Roddick (USA)	Bob Bryan (USA) & Mike Bryan (USA)
2002	Carlos Moya (ESP)	James Blake (USA) & Todd Martin (USA)
2001	Gustavo Kuerten (BRA)	Mahesh Bhupathi (IND) & Leander Paes (IND)
2000	Thomas Enqvist (SWE)	Todd Woodbridge (AUS) & Mark Woodforde (AUS)

(L-R) NENAD ZIMONJIC & DANIEL NESTOR

Draw: Singles-56 Doubles-24
Prize money: $2,430,000
Surface: Hard
Venue: Lindner Family Tennis Center
Tournament director: Bruce Flory
First held: 1899

OLYMPUS
US OPEN SERIES

Western & Southern
Financial Group®
MASTERS

MASTERS
1000
ATP
WORLD TOUR

TOURNAMENT WEBSITE:
www.cincytennis.com

ROGER FEDERER

ATP WORLD TOUR DOUBLES
FEEL THE INTENSITY

FEEL IT

FAST.
FURIOUS.
AND FIERCE.

EXPERIENCE THE DRAMA AS THE STARS BATTLE TO BECOME THE 2010 ATP WORLD TOUR DOUBLES CHAMPIONS

For the latest doubles information go to www.ATPWorldTour.com

AUGUST 22-28 | NEW HAVEN, CT, USA

PILOT PEN TENNIS

Sony Ericsson
WTA TOUR

OLYMPUS
US OPEN SERIES

PILOT PEN TENNIS at Yale

250
ATP WORLD TOUR

TOURNAMENT WEBSITE:
www.pilotpentennis.com

Draw: Singles-48 Doubles-16
Prize money: $663,750
Surface: Hard
Venue: Connecticut Tennis Center at Yale
Tournament director:
Anne Person Worcester
First held: 2005

©Matthew Stockman/Getty Images

A s the countdown to the US Open gathers pace, the week before the New York Grand Slam gets under way the stars of the ATP World Tour and Sony Ericsson WTA Tour head to Connecticut for the hard court Pilot Pen Tennis in New Haven. The event gives players their last opportunity to gather Olympus US Open Series points, a ten-tournament circuit that runs throughout the North American summer. American fans were given the chance to watch Spaniard Fernando Verdasco in the flesh in 2009 after the wild card entry into the draw went on to beat Sam Querrey in the final to earn his first ATP World Tour title of the year. American James Blake has the most New Haven trophies having won the event twice, while Russian Nikolay Davydenko and Croatia's Marin Cilic have also lifted the trophy.

PAST CHAMPIONS

YEAR	SINGLES	DOUBLES
2009	Fernando Verdasco (ESP)	Julian Knowle (AUT) & Jurgen Melzer (AUT)
2008	Marin Cilic (CRO)	Marcelo Melo (BRA) & Andre Sa (BRA)
2007	James Blake (USA)	Mahesh Bhupathi (IND) & Nenad Zimonjic (SRB)
2006	Nikolay Davydenko (RUS)	Jonathan Erlich (ISR) & Andy Ram (ISR)
2005	James Blake (USA)	Gaston Etlis (ARG) & Martin Rodriguez (ARG)

NUMBER CRUNCHING

2009 TOP 100 SOUTH AFRICAN AIRWAYS ATP RANKINGS BY COUNTRY

=1	France	12 players
=1	Spain	12 players
3	Germany	11 players
4	Argentina	9 players
5	USA	9 players
6	Italy	5 players
7	Russia	5 players
8	Croatia	4 players
=9	Belgium	3 players
=9	Serbia	3 players
=9	Switzerland	3 players

2009 SINGLES TITLES BY COUNTRY

1	Spain	13
2	Russia	7
=3	France	6
=3	Great Britain	6
=5	USA	5
=5	Serbia	5
=7	Argentina	4
=7	Switzerland	4
=9	Croatia	3
=9	Czech Republic	3

JO-WILFRIED TSONGA

©Mark Kolbe/AFP/Getty Images

AUGUST 30-SEPTEMBER 12 | FLUSHING MEADOWS, NEW YORK, USA

US OPEN

> New York City's US Open is a high-octane extravaganza of an event – the final Grand Slam on the calendar

The US Open, held at the USTA Billie Jean King National Tennis Center in Flushing Meadows at the end of August and beginning of September, is a high-octane extravaganza of a tennis event and the final Grand Slam of the year. The hard court tournament is known for its passionate crowds, dramatic and atmospheric night sessions and the biggest centre court in the world, the Arthur Ashe Stadium, which holds an incredible 23,771 fans.

Three players share top spot on the singles titles won during the Open era leaderboard – Jimmy Connors (1974, '76, '78, '82-83), Pete Sampras (1990, '93, '95-96, 2002) and Roger Federer who notched up an amazing five successive titles between 2004 and 2008.

Federer was denied a record-breaking sixth trophy in 2009 when he was shocked in the final by young Argentine Juan Martin Del Potro, who beat the Swiss star in five sets to land his first Grand Slam title. The South American became the fifth youngest player to lift the US Open trophy in the Open era and became the tallest Grand Slam winner at 6ft 6''. He also joined countryman Guillermo Vilas as the only South American champion in New York.

PAST **CHAMPIONS**

YEAR	SINGLES	DOUBLES
2009	Juan Martin Del Potro (ARG)	Lukas Dlouhy (CZE) & Leander Paes (IND)
2008	Roger Federer (SUI)	Bob Bryan (USA) & Mike Bryan (USA)
2007	Roger Federer (SUI)	Simon Aspelin (SWE) & Julian Knowle (AUT)
2006	Roger Federer (SUI)	Martin Damm (CZE) & Leander Paes (IND)
2005	Roger Federer (SUI)	Bob Bryan (USA) & Mike Bryan (USA)
2004	Roger Federer (SUI)	Mark Knowles (BAH) & Daniel Nestor (CAN)
2003	Andy Roddick (USA)	Jonas Bjorkman (SWE) & Todd Woodbridge (AUS)
2002	Pete Sampras (USA)	Mahesh Bhupathi (IND) & Max Mirnyi (BLR)
2001	Lleyton Hewitt (AUS)	Wayne Black (ZIM) & Kevin Ullyett (ZIM)
2000	Marat Safin (RUS)	Lleyton Hewitt (AUS) & Max Mirnyi (BLR)

(L-R) LUKAS DLOUHY & LEANDER PAES

Draw: Singles-128 Doubles-64
Prize money: TBD
Surface: Hard
Venue: USTA Billie Jean King National Tennis Center
Tournament director: Jim Curley
First held: 1881

GRAND SLAM®
(2000 POINTS)

TOURNAMENT WEBSITE:
www.usopen.org

JUAN MARTIN DEL POTRO

©Timothy A. Clary/AFP/Getty Images

SEPTEMBER 20-26 | METZ, FRANCE

OPEN DE MOSELLE

TOURNAMENT WEBSITE:
www.opendemoselle.com

Draw: Singles-28, Doubles-16	
Prize money: €398,250	
Surface: Indoor Hard	
Venue: Les Arènes de Metz	
Tournament director: Julien Boutter	
First held: 2003	

The first two editions of the Open de Moselle, an indoor hard court ATP World Tour 250 held in the so-called 'Green City' of Metz, in north-eastern France, was won by home-grown players with Arnaud Clement and Jerome Haehnel ruling in 2003 and 2004 respectively. Croatian Ivan Ljubicic, Serb Novak Djokovic, Russian Dmitry Tursunov and Spain's Tommy Robredo reigned between 2005 and 2008 before Gael Monfils re-instated French rule in 2009 when he beat Germany's Philipp Kohlschreiber in the final to end a personal title drought of four years. The doubles event has been dominated by the home favourites too with the trophy going to French teams for the first six years before Britons Ken Skupski and Colin Fleming got their hands on the silverware in 2009.

GAEL MONFILS

©Jean-Christophe Verhaegen/AFP/Getty Images

PAST CHAMPIONS

YEAR	SINGLES	DOUBLES
2009	Gael Monfils (FRA)	Colin Fleming (GBR) & Ken Skupski (GBR)
2008	Dmitry Tursunov (RUS)	Arnaud Clement (FRA) & Michael Llodra (FRA)
2007	Tommy Robredo (ESP)	Arnaud Clement (FRA) & Michael Llodra (FRA)
2006	Novak Djokovic (SRB)	Richard Gasquet (FRA) & Fabrice Santoro (FRA)
2005	Ivan Ljubicic (CRO)	Michael Llodra (FRA) & Fabrice Santoro (FRA)

SEPTEMBER 20-26 | BUCHAREST, ROMANIA

BCR OPEN ROMANIA

TOURNAMENT WEBSITE:
www.bcropenromania.ro

Draw: Singles-28, Doubles-16	
Prize money: €368,450	
Surface: Clay	
Venue: B.N.R. Arenas	
Tournament director: Bogdan Enoiu	
First held: 1996	

The BCR Open Romania is the final clay court tournament on the 2010 ATP World Tour calendar and gives those players who are dominant on the surface one last chance to grab another title before heading to compete in the Asian swing of events before going indoors for the remainder of the European winter. Frenchmen have done well at the event in recent years with Gilles Simon winning back-to-back titles in 2007 and 2008 but it was Spain's Albert Montanes who continued his excellent season in 2009 by winning his second title of the year in Bucharest following earlier success in Estoril, Portugal, in May. Those results enabled the Barcelona resident to finish the season with his highest-ever end-of-season ranking of No.31.

ALBERT MONTANES

©Chris Hyde/Getty Images

PAST CHAMPIONS

YEAR	SINGLES	DOUBLES
2009	Albert Montanes (ESP)	Frantisek Cermak (CZE) & Michal Mertinak (SVK)
2008	Gilles Simon (FRA)	Nicolas Devilder (FRA) & Paul-Henri Mathieu (FRA)
2007	Gilles Simon (FRA)	Oliver Marach (AUT) & Michal Mertinak (SVK)
2006	Jurgen Melzer (AUT)	Mariusz Fyrstenberg (POL) & Marcin Matkowski (POL)
2005	Florent Serra (FRA)	Jose Acasuso (URU) & Sebastian Prieto (ARG)

SEPTEMBER 27-OCTOBER 3 | KUALA LUMPUR, MALAYSIA

PROTON MALAYSIAN OPEN

TOURNAMENT WEBSITE:
www.MalaysianOpenTennis.com

Draw: Singles-28 Doubles-16
Prize money: $850,000
Surface: Indoor Hard
Venue: Putra Stadium, Bukit Jalil
Tournament director: Nick Freyer
First held: 2009

NIKOLAY DAVYDENKO

The Proton Malaysian Open is one of the newest tournaments on the ATP World Tour calendar after the inaugural staging of the event in 2009. The indoor hard court ATP World Tour 250 held at the 16,000-seat Putra Stadium, together with the PTT Thailand Open in Bangkok the same week, marks the beginning of the three-week Asian swing of tournaments that sees the best players in the world visit Malaysia, Thailand, Japan and China where the mini circuit comes to a climax at the Shanghai ATP Masters 1000, Presented by Rolex. Nikolay Davydenko continued his excellent season when he became the first ever singles champion in Kuala Lumpur after beating Spain's Fernando Verdasco 64 75 in the final and the Russian went on to enjoy a fantastic stay in the region by winning his third ATP World Tour Masters 1000 title in Shanghai two weeks later.

(L-R) MARCIN MATKOWSKI & MARIUSZ FYRSTENBERG

PAST CHAMPIONS

YEAR	SINGLES	DOUBLES
2009	Nikolay Davydenko (RUS)	Mariusz Fyrstenberg (POL) & Marcin Matkowski (POL)

SEPTEMBER 27-OCTOBER 3 | BANGKOK, THAILAND

PTT THAILAND OPEN

TOURNAMENT WEBSITE:
www.pttthailandopen.org

Draw: Singles-28, Doubles-16
Prize money: $551,000
Surface: Hard
Venue: Impact Arena
Tournament director: Allon Khakshouri
First held: 2003

GILLES SIMON

The eight-year-old PTT Thailand Open has welcomed some of the game's household names since it was first held in Bangkok in 2003. The Impact Arena's hard courts seem to favour attacking players and the likes of Roger Federer, Jo-Wilfried Tsonga, James Blake and Taylor Dent have all won the ATP World Tour 250 event over the years. In 2009 it was Frenchman Gilles Simon who hit top form, beating Serbia's Viktor Troicki in the final to win his first singles trophy of the year. During his stay in the Thai capital, Simon, along with fellow pros Robby Ginepri and John Isner, also got the chance to try his hand at some martial arts – Thai Boxing to be exact – when the trio were given lessons from Olympic champion Summit Jongjorhor.

PAST CHAMPIONS

YEAR	SINGLES	DOUBLES
2009	Gilles Simon (FRA)	Eric Butorac (USA) & Rajeev Ram (USA)
2008	Jo-Wilfried Tsonga (FRA)	Lukas Dlouhy (CZE) & Leander Paes (IND)
2007	Dmitry Tursunov (RUS)	Sanchai Ratiwatana (THA) & Sonchat Ratiwatana (THA)
2006	James Blake (USA)	Jonathan Erlich (ISR) & Andy Ram (ISR)
2005	Roger Federer (SUI)	Paul Hanley (AUS) & Leander Paes (IND)

OCTOBER 4-10 | BEIJING, CHINA

CHINA OPEN

TOURNAMENT WEBSITE:
www.chinaopen.com.cn

Draw: Singles-32 Doubles-16
Prize money: $2,100,000
Surface: Hard
Venue: National Tennis Centre
Tournament director: Mr Zhang Junhui (Alfred)
First held: 2004

In early October, Beijing welcomes the best men and women in the world when the combined ATP World Tour 500 and Sony Ericsson WTA Tour China Open bursts into life at the Beijing Olympic Green Tennis Center, purpose-built for the 2008 Olympic Games. The event holds an important slot in the calendar, in the middle of the autumn Asian Swing which comes to a climax at the Shanghai ATP Masters 1000, Presented by Rolex a week later.

The futuristic Olympic Green Tennis Center boasts 10 courts, including three main show courts designed to represent lotus flowers – an emblem of the 2008 Beijing Olympics. The facilities attract some of the best players in the world each year and it was Serbian Novak Djokovic who ended the week as champion in 2009 when he defeated Croatian Marin Cilic in the final.

The tournament began in 1994 when American Michael Chang became its first ever champion. Over the years four world No.1s – Jim Courier, Marat Safin, Rafael Nadal and Andy Roddick – have all had their hands on the Beijing trophy.

NOVAK DJOKOVIC

BEIJING

(L-R) MIKE BRYAN & BOB BRYAN

PAST **CHAMPIONS**

YEAR	SINGLES	DOUBLES
2009	Novak Djokovic (SRB)	Bob Bryan (USA) & Mike Bryan (USA)
2008	Andy Roddick (USA)	Stephen Huss (AUS) & Ross Hutchins (GBR)
2007	Fernando Gonzalez (CHI)	Rik De Voest (RSA) & Ashley Fisher (AUS)
2006	Marcos Baghdatis (CYP)	Mario Ancic (CRO) & Mahesh Bhupathi (IND)
2005	Rafael Nadal (ESP)	Justin Gimelstob (USA) & Nathan Healey (AUS)
2004	Marat Safin (RUS)	Justin Gimelstob (USA) & Graydon Oliver (USA)
1997	Jim Courier (USA)	Mahesh Bhupathi (IND) & Leander Paes (IND)
1996	Greg Rusedski (GBR)	Martin Damm (CZE) & Andrei Olhovskiy (RUS)
1995	Michael Chang (USA)	Tommy Ho (USA) & Sebastien Lareau (CAN)
1994	Michael Chang (USA)	Tommy Ho (USA) & Kent Kinnear (USA)

» **TICKET INFO:** Call +81-3-3481-2511 or visit jta-tennis.or.jp

OCTOBER 4-10 | TOKYO, JAPAN

RAKUTEN JAPAN OPEN

ⓡ **Rakuten OPEN**

TOURNAMENT WEBSITE:
jta-tennis.or.jp

Draw: Singles-32 Doubles-16
Prize money: $1,100,000
Surface: Hard
Venue: Ariake Tennis Colosseum and Ariake Tennis Forest Park
Tournament director: Nao Kawatei
First held: 1972

Tokyo welcomes the best players in the world when it stages the Rakuten Japan Open, which dates back to 1973, making it the longest-running ATP World Tour event in Asia. The tournament has a wonderfully relaxed feel with the match courts and the main show court – the Ariake Tennis Colosseum – set inside the Ariake Tennis Forest Park, a wooded area which boasts 48 courts in total. The main action takes place in the 10,000-seat Colosseum, which was one of the first tennis arenas to have a retractable roof. This prestigious trophy features almost every one of the game's legends, including Ken Rosewall who won the first staging of the event back in 1973, Pete Sampras, John McEnroe, Roger Federer and Swede Stefan Edberg, who has the most titles – four in five years between 1987 and 1991. At last year's event nothing could halt Frenchman Jo-Wilfried Tsonga, who was in unstoppable form, blowing away fellow countryman Gael Monfils in the semi-finals and then Russian Mikhail Youzhny in the final to land the fifth title of his career.

JO-WILFRIED TSONGA

PAST **CHAMPIONS**

YEAR	SINGLES	DOUBLES
2009	Jo-Wilfried Tsonga (FRA)	Julian Knowle (AUT) & Jurgen Melzer (AUT)
2008	Tomas Berdych (CZE)	Mikhail Youzhny (RUS) & Mischa Zverev (GER)
2007	David Ferrer (ESP)	Jordan Kerr (AUS) & Robert Lindstedt (SWE)
2006	Roger Federer (SUI)	Ashley Fisher (AUS) & Tripp Phillips (USA)
2005	Wesley Moodie RSA)	Satoshi Iwabuchi (JPN) & Takao Suzuki (JPN)
2004	Jiri Novak (CZE)	Jared Palmer (USA) & Pavel Vizner (CZE)
2003	Rainer Schuettler (GER)	Justin Gimelstob (USA) & Nicolas Kiefer (GER)
2002	Kenneth Carlsen (DEN)	Jeff Coetzee (RSA) & Chris Haggard (RSA)
2001	Lleyton Hewitt (AUS)	Rick Leach (USA) & David Macpherson (AUS)
2000	Sjeng Schalken (NED)	Mahesh Bhupathi (IND) & Leander Paes (IND)

OCTOBER 10-17 | SHANGHAI, CHINA

SHANGHAI ATP
MASTERS 1000 PRESENTED
BY ROLEX

ATP WORLD TOUR
MASTERS 1000

NIKOLAY DAVYDENKO

©Matthew Stockman/Getty Images

Draw: Singles-56 Doubles-24
Prize money: $3,240,000
Surface: Hard
Venue: Qizhong Tennis Center
Tournament directors: Michael Luevano and Leon Sun
First held: 2009

TOURNAMENT WEBSITE:
www.jussevent.com

In 2009 Shanghai became the eighth ATP World Tour Masters 1000 stop on the calendar

(L-R)JULIEN BENNETEAU & JO-WILFRIED TSONGA

Shanghai joined an elite group of cities in 2009 when it staged its first ever ATP World Tour Masters 1000 event, which brought to a climax the three-week Asian swing of tournaments held in September and October. Previously, the Chinese city had staged the end-of-season ATP Tennis Masters Cup and in 2009 it became the eighth ATP World Tour Masters 1000 stop on the calendar when the best 56 players in the world assembled at the Qizhong Tennis Center, which features a 15,000-capacity main show court. The first ever staging of the event also coincided with the opening of a brand new second show court, which can seat another 5,000 fans.

The inaugural event featured some intriguing story lines and it was Russian Nikolay Davydenko who was the first man to etch his name onto the brand new trophy when he scored back-to-back victories over Novak Djokovic and Rafael Nadal to claim the third ATP World Tour Masters 1000 title of his career. The first doubles team to taste glory in Shanghai were French pair Julien Benneteau and Jo-Wilfried Tsonga, who collected their first ATP World Tour title together with a 6-2, 6-4 victory over Poles Mariusz Fyrstenberg and Marcin Matkowski.

PAST CHAMPIONS

YEAR	SINGLES	DOUBLES
2009	Nikolay Davydenko (RUS)	Julien Benneteau (FRA) & Jo-Wilfried Tsonga (FRA)

OCTOBER 18-24 | STOCKHOLM, SWEDEN

IF STOCKHOLM OPEN

TOURNAMENT WEBSITE:
www.ifstockholmopen.se

Draw: Singles-28, Doubles-16
Prize money: €531,000
Surface: Indoor Hard
Venue: Kungliga Tennishallen (Royal Tennis Hall)
Tournament director: Thomas Johansson
First held: 1969

Together with the Kremlin Cup in Moscow (see below), the If Stockholm Open begins the final group of indoor European tournaments that lead up to the Barclays ATP World Tour Finals in London in late November. The event dates back to 1969 and has been staged at the indoor Kungliga Tennishallen for the majority of its existence, except between 1989 and 1994 when it was held at the city's Globe Arena. Some of the Swedish greats have won the title over the years – Bjorn Borg in 1980, Mats Wilander in 1983 and Stefan Edberg won back-to-back titles in 1986 and 1987. Cypriot Marcos Baghdatis was the latest player to etch his name onto the honour roll when he capped a fine week by beating Olivier Rochus of Belgium 61 75 in the 2009 final.

MARCOS BAGHDATIS

PAST CHAMPIONS

YEAR	SINGLES	DOUBLES
2009	Marcos Baghdatis (CYP)	Bruno Soares (BRA) & Kevin Ullyett (ZIM)
2008	David Nalbandian (ARG)	Jonas Bjorkman (SWE) & Kevin Ullyett (ZIM)
2007	Ivo Karlovic (CRO)	Jonas Bjorkman (SWE) & Max Mirnyi (BLR)
2006	James Blake (USA)	Paul Hanley (AUS) & Kevin Ullyett (ZIM)
2005	James Blake (USA)	Wayne Arthurs (AUS) & Paul Hanley (AUS)

OCTOBER 18-24 | MOSCOW, RUSSIA

ATP KREMLIN CUP

TOURNAMENT WEBSITE:
www.kremlincup.ru

Draw: Singles-28, Doubles-16
Prize money: $1,000,000
Surface: Indoor hard
Venue: Olympic Stadium
Tournament director: Amir Tarpischev
First held: 1990

Every October the men and women of the tour head to one of the most dramatic cities in the world for the combined ATP World Tour and Sony Ericsson WTA Tour Kremlin Cup which will celebrate its 21st year in 2010. Played indoors at the gigantic Olympic Stadium in the north of the city, the event became the country's first professional international tournament when it was first held in 1990. Russia's players have made the most of home advantage with the trophy going to home-grown players in 14 of the 20 years the event has been played. Former world No.1 Yevgeny Kafelnikov has been by far the most successful at the tournament, claiming five successive titles between 1997 and 2001. In 2009 another Russian ruled when Mikhail Youzhny beat Serbia's Janko Tipsarevic in the final.

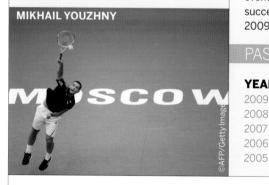

MIKHAIL YOUZHNY

PAST CHAMPIONS

YEAR	SINGLES	DOUBLES
2009	Mikhail Youzhny (RUS)	Pablo Cuevas (URU) & Marcel Granollers (ESP)
2008	Igor Kunitsyn (RUS)	Sergiy Stakhovsky (UKR) & Potito Starace (ITA)
2007	Nikolay Davydenko (RUS)	Marat Safin (RUS) & Dmitry Tursunov (RUS)
2006	Nikolay Davydenko (RUS)	Fabrice Santoro (FRA) & Nenad Zimonjic (SRB)
2005	Igor Andreev (RUS)	Max Mirnyi (BLR) & Mikhail Youzhny (RUS)

OCTOBER 25-31 | LYON, FRANCE

GRAND PRIX DE TENNIS DE LYON

Grand Prix de Tennis de Lyon

TOURNAMENT WEBSITE:
www.gptennislyon.com

Draw:	Singles-28 Doubles-16
Prize money:	€575,250
Surface:	Indoor Hard
Venue:	Palais des Sports Lyon Gerland
Tournament director:	Gilles Moretton
First held:	1987

IVAN LJUBICIC

©Philippe Merle/AFP/Getty Images

The second-largest city in France hosts the best in the world when the Grand Prix de Tennis de Lyon gets under way at the Palais des Sports Lyon Gerland indoor arena every October. A popular stop on the European winter indoor swing, the ATP World Tour 250 event began in 1987 and has some real legends on its role of honour. French favourite Yannick Noah was the first ever champion, and the likes of John McEnroe, Pete Sampras, Yevgeny Kafelnikov, Robin Soderling and Andy Roddick have all won in the city famous for its gastronomy. One of the older players on the tour, Croatia's Ivan Ljubicic, hit some red-hot form at last year's event, beating Frenchman Michael Llodra in the final to become only the third thirtysomething to win an ATP World Tour singles title in 2009.

PAST**CHAMPIONS**

YEAR	SINGLES	DOUBLES
2009	Ivan Ljubicic (CRO)	Julien Benneteau (FRA) & Nicolas Mahut (FRA)
2008	Robin Soderling (SWE)	Michael Llodra (FRA) & Andy Ram (ISR)
2007	Sebastien Grosjean (FRA)	Sebastien Grosjean (FRA) & Jo-Wilfried Tsonga (FRA)
2006	Richard Gasquet (FRA)	Julien Benneteau (FRA) & Arnaud Clement (FRA)
2005	Andy Roddick (USA)	Michael Llodra (FRA) & Fabrice Santoro (FRA)

OPEN ERA RECORDS

* Records taken between 1968 and 2009

JOHN McENROE

©Chris Cole/Getty Images

FABRICE SANTORO

©Kiyoshi Ota/Getty Images

RECORD	PLAYER	STATISTIC	YEAR
Match wins streak	Guillermo Vilas (ARG)	46	1977
Singles titles won	Guillermo Vilas (ARG)	16	1977
Doubles titles won	John McEnroe (USA)	17	1979
Doubles titles won by team	John McEnroe (USA) & Peter Fleming (USA)	15	1979
Match winning %	John McEnroe (USA)	.965 (82-3)	1984
Prize money won	**Roger Federer** (SUI)	$10,130,620	2007
Youngest title winner	Aaron Krickstein (USA)	16 yrs, 2 mths	1983 (Tel Aviv)
Oldest title winner	Pancho Gonzalez (USA)	43 yrs, 9 mths	1972 (Des Moines)
Lowest ranked title winner	**Lleyton Hewitt** (AUS)	No.550	1998 (Adelaide)
Longest singles match	Fabrice Santoro (FRA) V **Arnaud Clement** (FRA)	6 hrs, 33 mins	2004 (Roland Garros)

NUMBER CRUNCHING

OCTOBER 25-31 | VIENNA, AUSTRIA

BANK AUSTRIA TENNISTROPHY

TOURNAMENT WEBSITE:
www.bankaustria-tennistrophy.at

Draw: Singles-32 Doubles-16
Prize money: €575,250
Surface: Indoor Hard
Venue: Wiener Stadthalle
Tournament director: Herwig Straka
First held: 1974

JURGEN MELZER

Austria's picturesque capital city is the venue for one of two events held during the same week in late October that bring the ATP World Tour 250 circuit to a close. A glance down the list of The Bank Austria TennisTrophy's former champions and it is clear that the indoor tournament has been supported by some of the best players in the world since it began in 1974. Vitas Gerulaitis, Stan Smith, Ivan Lendl, Goran Ivanisevic, Andre Agassi, Boris Becker, Pete Sampras and Roger Federer have all tasted victory in Vienna but one of the most popular champions will have been the man who won the title in 2009. Jurgen Melzer ended a 21-year wait for a home-grown champion when he beat top seed Marin Cilic 64 63 in last year's final. Melzer became the first Austrian winner since Horst Skoff in 1988.

PAST**CHAMPIONS**

YEAR	SINGLES	DOUBLES
2009	Jurgen Melzer (AUT)	Lukasz Kubot (POL) & Oliver Marach (AUT)
2008	Philipp Petzschner (GER)	Max Mirnyi (BLR) & Andy Ram (ISR)
2007	Novak Djokovic (SRB)	Mariusz Fyrstenberg (POL) & Marcin Matkowski (POL)
2006	Ivan Ljubicic (CRO)	Petr Pala (CZE) & Pavel Vizner (CZE)
2005	Ivan Ljubicic (CRO)	Mark Knowles (BAH) & Daniel Nestor (CAN)

OCTOBER 24-31 | ST. PETERSBURG, RUSSIA

ST. PETERSBURG OPEN

TOURNAMENT WEBSITE:
www.spbopen.ru

Draw: Singles-28, Doubles-16
Prize money: $663,750
Surface: Indoor Hard
Venue: SCC Peterburgsky
Tournament director: Mikhail Rydnik
First held: 1995

SERGIY STAKHOVSKY

The stars of the game get the chance to visit another of the most beautiful cities in the world when the tour stops in Russia for the St. Petersburg Open in late October. The indoor hard court ATP World Tour 250 event was first held in 1995 and the Russian fans have enjoyed cheering four home-grown champions to victory in the last 15 years. Yevgeny Kafelnikov was the first back in 1995, before Marat Safin claimed back-to-back trophies in 2000 and 2001. Mikhail Youzhny became the latest Russian to add his name to the list in 2004. Last year's event threw up a surprise champion when Ukrainian World No.93 Sergiy Stakhovsky became the third qualifier to win an ATP World Tour title in 2009 by seeing off unseeded Argentine Horacio Zeballos in the final.

PAST **CHAMPIONS**

YEAR	SINGLES	DOUBLES
2009	Sergiy Stakhovsky (UKR)	Colin Fleming (GBR) & Ken Skupski (GBR)
2008	Andy Murray (GBR)	Travis Parrott (USA) & Filip Polasek (SVK)
2007	Andy Murray (GBR)	Daniel Nestor (CAN) & Nenad Zimonjic (SRB)
2006	Mario Ancic (CRO)	Simon Aspelin (SWE) & Todd Perry (AUS)
2005	Thomas Johansson (SWE)	Julian Knowle (AUT) & Jurgen Melzer (AUT)

Have you got what it takes to be a Barclays Ball Kid?

The search is on for thirty talented young people to join the best on court as ball kids at the Barclays ATP World Tour Finals 2010 in London.

Visit www.barclaysballkids.com to find out more

Competition open exclusively to 12–16 year olds who are registered by a Barclays customer.

Online entries for 2010 close on 25 Feb 2010. If you have missed this year's application deadline, register online to find out about your chance to be a Barclays Ball Kid in 2011.

Barclays is proud to be title sponsor of the ATP World Tour Finals from 2009 to 2013.

NOVEMBER 1-7 | BASEL, SWITZERLAND

DAVIDOFF SWISS INDOORS BASEL

TOURNAMENT WEBSITE:
www.davidoffswissindoors.ch

Draw: Singles-32 Doubles-16
Prize money: €1,225,000
Surface: Indoor hard
Venue: St. Jakobshalle
Tournament director:
Roger Brennwald
First held: 1970

Since it was established in 1970, the Davidoff Swiss Indoors Basel has become one of the most important indoor tournaments on the calendar and it still attracts the best players in the world as one of 11 ATP World Tour 500 events. In some ways the tournament can claim to have played a part in the development of arguably the game's greatest ever player since Roger Federer was given his first taste of the big time at his hometown event as a ball boy. The Swiss returned years later to claim three titles between 2006 and 2008.

Federer is one of a host of big names to have ruled at St. Jakobshalle since the early 70s where Bjorn Borg, Ivan Lendl, John McEnroe, Boris Becker, Stefan Edberg and Pete Sampras have all added their names to the roll of honour. Federer was denied his fourth Basel trophy in 2009, however, when Serbian Novak Djokovic spoiled the party for the locals by beating the home favourite in three sets to earn his first title in the picturesque Swiss city.

NOVAK DJOKOVIC

©Julian Finney/Getty Images

(L-R) NENAD ZIMONJIC & DANIEL NESTOR

©Julian Finney/Getty Images

PAST **CHAMPIONS**

YEAR	SINGLES	DOUBLES
2009	Novak Djokovic (SRB)	Daniel Nestor (CAN) & Nenad Zimonjic (SRB)
2008	Roger Federer (SUI)	Mahesh Bhupathi (IND) & Mark Knowles (BAH)
2007	Roger Federer (SUI)	Bob Bryan (USA) & Mike Bryan (USA)
2006	Roger Federer (SUI)	Mark Knowles (BAH) & Daniel Nestor (CAN)
2005	Fernando Gonzalez (CHI)	Agustin Calleri (ARG) & Fernando Gonzalez (CHI)
2004	Jiri Novak (CZE)	Bob Bryan (USA) & Mike Bryan (USA)
2003	Guillermo Coria (ARG)	Mark Knowles (BAH) & Daniel Nestor (CAN)
2002	David Nalbandian (ARG)	Bob Bryan (USA) & Mike Bryan (USA)
2001	Tim Henman (GBR)	Ellis Ferreira (RSA) & Rick Leach (USA)
2000	Thomas Enqvist (SWE)	Donald Johnson (USA) & Piet Norval (RSA)

» TICKET INFO: Visit www.valenciaopen500.com

NOVEMBER 1-7 | VALENCIA, SPAIN

VALENCIA OPEN 500

TOURNAMENT WEBSITE:
www.valenciaopen500.com

Draw: Singles-32 Doubles-16
Prize money: €1,357,000
Surface: Indoor hard
Venue: Ciudad de las Artes y las Ciencas Valencia
Tournament director: Antonio Martinez Cascales
First held: 2003

The Valencia tournament began as an outdoor spring clay court event in 2003 before changing status, venue, surface and its place in the calendar in 2009. The tournament became one of 11 ATP World Tour 500s and home to one of the most impressive stadiums on the tour in 2009 when it was held in early November as an indoor hard court tournament inside the brand new Agora building at the futuristic City of Arts and Sciences. With its new calendar position, the Valencia Open 500 will each year serve as a prime battleground for qualification for the season-ending Barclays ATP World Tour Finals.

During the early years the home-grown players dominated with Juan Carlos Ferrero (who now part-owns the tournament), Fernando Verdasco, two-time champion Nicolas Almagro and David Ferrer all claiming the title on clay. In 2009 Great Britain's Andy Murray ruled at the new venue, beating Verdasco in the last four before outplaying Russia's Mikhail Youzhny in the final to claim his sixth title of 2009.

ANDY MURRAY

(L-R) FRANTISEK CERMAK & MICHAL MERTINAK

PAST **CHAMPIONS**

YEAR	SINGLES	DOUBLES
2009	Andy Murray (GBR)	Frantisek Cermak (CZE) & Michal Mertinak (SVK)
2008	David Ferrer (ESP)	Maximo Gonzalez (ARG) & Juan Monaco (ARG)
2007	Nicolas Almagro (ESP)	Wesley Moodie (RSA) & Todd Perry (AUS)
2006	Nicolas Almagro (ESP)	David Skoch (CZE) & Tomas Zib (CZE)
2005	Igor Andreev (RUS)	Fernando Gonzalez (CHI) & Martin Rodriguez (ARG)
2004	Fernando Verdasco (ESP)	Gaston Etlis (ARG) & Martin Rodriguez (ARG)
2003	Juan Carlos Ferrero (ESP)	Lucas Arnold Ker (ARG) & Mariano Hood (ARG)

NOVEMBER 7-14 | PARIS, FRANCE

BNP PARIBAS MASTERS

" The Paris event holds extra significance since it often decides the final places up for grabs at the year-end championships "

The BNP Paribas Masters is the ninth and final ATP World Tour Masters 1000 event of the season and is another major tournament that boasts a long and illustrious roll of honour since it was first staged in 1986. This event holds even greater significance because of its position in the calendar as almost every year during the French event the remaining places up for grabs at the end-of-season Barclays ATP World Tour Finals are decided.

Germany's Boris Becker holds two of the tournament's records – he and Russian Marat Safin have the most titles after both won the French event three times, with Safin's titles all coming in a five-year period. Becker can also boast to be the youngest ever winner at the Palais Omnisports indoor arena in Bercy after his 1986 success came when he was just 18 years and 11 months old.

In 2009 Serbia's Novak Djokovic broke French hearts when he edged out home favourite Gael Monfils 62 57 76(3) in a dramatic final that lasted two hours and 43 minutes. The French fans have enjoyed cheering on two home grown players to glory in recent years, however, when Jo-Wilfried Tsonga won the event in 2008 and Sebastien Grosjean ruled in 2001.

(L-R) NOVAK DJOKOVIC & GAEL MONFILS

PAST CHAMPIONS

(L-R) NENAD ZIMONJIC & DANIEL NESTOR

YEAR	SINGLES	DOUBLES
2009	Novak Djokovic (SRB)	Daniel Nestor (CAN) & Nenad Zimonjic (FRA)
2008	Jo-Wilfried Tsonga (FRA)	Jonas Bjorkman (SWE) & Kevin Ullyett (ZIM)
2007	David Nalbandian (ARG)	Arnaud Clement (FRA) & Michael Llodra (FRA)
2006	Nikolay Davydenko (RUS)	Arnaud Clement (FRA) & Michael Llodra (FRA)
2005	Tomas Berdych (CZE)	Bob Bryan (USA) & Mike Bryan (USA)
2004	Marat Safin (RUS)	Jonas Bjorkman (SWE) & Todd Woodbridge (AUS)
2003	Tim Henman (GBR)	Wayne Arthurs (AUS) & Paul Hanley (AUS)
2002	Marat Safin (RUS)	Nicolas Escude (FRA) & Fabrice Santoro (FRA)
2001	Sebastien Grosjean (FRA)	Ellis Ferreira (RSA) & Rick Leach (USA)
2000	Marat Safin (RUS)	Nicklas Kulti (SWE) & Max Mirnyi (BLR)

Draw: Singles-48 Doubles-24
Prize money: €2,227,500
Surface: Indoor hard
Venue: Palais Omnisports de Paris-Bercy
Tournament director: Jean-François Caujolle
First held: 1986

TOURNAMENT WEBSITE:
www.bnpparibasmasters.com

NOVAK DJOKOVIC

© AFP/Getty Images

NOVEMBER 21-28 | LONDON, ENGLAND

BARCLAYS ATP WORLD TOUR FINALS

NIKOLAY DAVYDENKO

Julian Finney/Getty Images

Draw: Singles-8 Doubles-8
Prize money: $5,070,000
Surface: Indoor Hard
Venue: The O2
Tournament director: Brad Drewett
First held: 1970

TOURNAMENT WEBSITE:
www.BarclaysATPWorldTourFinals.com

> Federer is just one behind all-time title winners Lendl and Sampras who have each won the prestigious event five times

Every November the best eight singles players and the top eight doubles teams compete at the Barclays ATP World Tour Finals which will be held for the second time at The O2 in London in 2010. The event had travelled to all four corners of the world before moving to London in 2009 for the first of a five-year residency.

Pete Sampras and Ivan Lendl collected the most trophies during their years on the tour, both winning the event five times. Roger Federer is within touching distance on four and will be hoping to qualify once more in 2010 to give himself a chance of equalling Sampras and Lendl's record.

The tournament's first visit to London in 2009 was a huge success with record crowds enjoying the action from the first day until the last. The final featured US Open champion Juan Martin Del Potro against Nikolay Davydenko, who put out Federer in the semi-finals, and it was the Russian who went on to pick up the trophy with a straight-sets victory in front of another 17,500 sell-out crowd.

The doubles final saw Americans Bob and Mike Bryan collect their third season-ending championships title and in doing so were crowned ATP World Tour Doubles Champions for the fifth time in seven years.

PAST CHAMPIONS

BRYAN BROTHERS

YEAR	SINGLES	DOUBLES
2009	Nikolay Davydenko (RUS)	Bob Bryan (USA) & Mike Bryan (USA)
2008	Novak Djokovic (SRB)	Daniel Nestor (CAN) & Nenad Zimonjic (SRB)
2007	Roger Federer (SUI)	Mark Knowles (BAH) & Daniel Nestor (CAN)
2006	Roger Federer (SUI)	Jonas Bjorkman (SWE) & Max Mirnyi (BLR)
2005	David Nalbandian (ARG)	Michael Llodra (FRA) & Fabrice Santoro (FRA)
2004	Roger Federer (SUI)	Bob Bryan (USA) & Mike Bryan (USA)
2003	Roger Federer (SUI)	Bob Bryan (USA) & Mike Bryan (USA)
2002	Lleyton Hewitt (AUS)	EVENT NOT HELD
2001	Lleyton Hewitt (AUS)	Ellis Ferreira (RSA) & Rick Leach (USA)
2000	Gustavo Kuerten (BRA)	Donald Johnson (USA) & Piet Norval (RSA)

BARCLAYS

ATP
WORLD TOUR
FINALS

21–28 NOVEMBER 2010
REGISTER NOW FOR

BARCLAYS | ATP WOR

The stars will battle all year around the world to earn their place. Don't miss your chance to join them.